Release Management
Complete Self-Assessm

MW01711436

The guidance in this Self-Asse
best practices and standards in business process architecture, design
and quality management. The guidance is also based on the professional judgment of the individual collaborators listed in the Acknowledgments.

http://theartofservice.com
service@theartofservice.com

Table of Contents

About The Art of Service

The Art of Service, Business Process Architects since 2000, is dedicated to helping stakeholders achieve excellence.

Defining, designing, creating, and implementing a process to solve a stakeholders challenge or meet an objective is the most valuable role… In EVERY group, company, organization and department.

Unless you're talking a one-time, single-use project, there should be a process. Whether that process is managed and implemented by humans, AI, or a combination of the two, it needs to be designed by someone with a complex enough perspective to ask the right questions.

Someone capable of asking the right questions and step back and say, 'What are we really trying to accomplish here? And is there a different way to look at it?'

With The Art of Service's Standard Requirements Self-Assessments, we empower people who can do just that — whether their title is marketer, entrepreneur, manager, salesperson, consultant, Business Process Manager, executive assistant, IT Manager, CIO etc... —they are the people who rule the future. They are people who watch the process as it happens, and ask the right questions to make the process work better.

Contact us when you need any support with this Self-Assessment and any help with templates, blue-prints and examples of standard documents you might need:

http://theartofservice.com
service@theartofservice.com

Acknowledgments

This checklist was developed under the auspices of The Art of Service, chaired by Gerardus Blokdyk.

Representatives from several client companies participated in the preparation of this Self-Assessment.

In addition, we are thankful for the design and printing services provided.

Included Resources - how to access

Included with your purchase of the book is the Release Management Self-Assessment Spreadsheet Dashboard which contains all questions and Self-Assessment areas and auto-generates insights, graphs, and project RACI planning - all with examples to get you started right away.

How? Simply send an email to
access@theartofservice.com
with this books' title in the subject to get the Release Management Self Assessment Tool right away.

You will receive the following contents with New and Updated specific criteria:

- The latest quick edition of the book in PDF
- The latest complete edition of the book in PDF, which criteria correspond to the criteria in...
- The Self-Assessment Excel Dashboard, and...
- Example pre-filled Self-Assessment Excel Dashboard to get familiar with results generation
- In-depth specific Checklists covering the topic
- Project management checklists and templates to assist with implementation

INCLUDES LIFETIME SELF ASSESSMENT UPDATES

Every self assessment comes with Lifetime Updates and Lifetime Free Updated Books. Lifetime Updates is an industry-first feature which allows you to receive verified self assessment updates, ensuring you always have the most accurate information at your fingertips.

Get it now- you will be glad you did - do it now, before you forget.

Send an email to **access@theartofservice.com** with this books' title in the subject to get the Release Management Self Assessment Tool right away.

Your feedback is invaluable to us

If you recently bought this book, we would love to hear from you! You can do this by writing a review on amazon (or the online store where you purchased this book) about your last purchase! As part of our continual service improvement process, we love to hear real client experiences and feedback.

How does it work?
To post a review on Amazon, just log in to your account and click on the Create Your Own Review button (under Customer Reviews) of the relevant product page. You can find examples of product reviews in Amazon. If you purchased from another online store, simply follow their procedures.

What happens when I submit my review?
Once you have submitted your review, send us an email at review@theartofservice.com with the link to your review so we can properly thank you for your feedback.

Purpose of this Self-Assessment

This Self-Assessment has been developed to improve understanding of the requirements and elements of Release Management, based on best practices and standards in business process architecture, design and quality management.

It is designed to allow for a rapid Self-Assessment to determine how closely existing management practices and procedures correspond to the elements of the Self-Assessment.

The criteria of requirements and elements of Release Management have been rephrased in the format of a Self-Assessment questionnaire, with a seven-criterion scoring system, as explained in this document.

In this format, even with limited background knowledge of

Release Management, a manager can quickly review existing operations to determine how they measure up to the standards. This in turn can serve as the starting point of a 'gap analysis' to identify management tools or system elements that might usefully be implemented in the organization to help improve overall performance.

How to use the Self-Assessment

On the following pages are a series of questions to identify to what extent your Release Management initiative is complete in comparison to the requirements set in standards.

To facilitate answering the questions, there is a space in front of each question to enter a score on a scale of '1' to '5'.

1 Strongly Disagree

2 Disagree

3 Neutral

4 Agree

5 Strongly Agree

Read the question and rate it with the following in front of mind:

**'In my belief,
the answer to this question is clearly defined'.**

There are two ways in which you can choose to interpret this statement;

1. how aware are you that the answer to the question is clearly defined
2. for more in-depth analysis you can choose to gather

evidence and confirm the answer to the question. This obviously will take more time, most Self-Assessment users opt for the first way to interpret the question and dig deeper later on based on the outcome of the overall Self-Assessment.

A score of '1' would mean that the answer is not clear at all, where a '5' would mean the answer is crystal clear and defined. Leave emtpy when the question is not applicable or you don't want to answer it, you can skip it without affecting your score. Write your score in the space provided.

After you have responded to all the appropriate statements in each section, compute your average score for that section, using the formula provided, and round to the nearest tenth. Then transfer to the corresponding spoke in the Release Management Scorecard on the second next page of the Self-Assessment.

Your completed Release Management Scorecard will give you a clear presentation of which Release Management areas need attention.

Release Management Scorecard Example

Example of how the finalized Scorecard can look like:

Release Management Scorecard

Your Scores:

BEGINNING OF THE SELF-ASSESSMENT:

CRITERION #1: RECOGNIZE

INTENT: Be aware of the need for change. Recognize that there is an unfavorable variation, problem or symptom.

In my belief, the answer to this question is clearly defined:

5 Strongly Agree

4 Agree

3 Neutral

2 Disagree

1 Strongly Disagree

1. What activities does the governance board need to consider?
<--- Score

2. Are there recognized Release Management problems?
<--- Score

3. Do you know what you need to know about

Release Management?
<--- Score

4. How can auditing be a preventative security measure?
<--- Score

5. Who needs what information?
<--- Score

6. Will a response program recognize when a crisis occurs and provide some level of response?
<--- Score

7. Does Release Management create potential expectations in other areas that need to be recognized and considered?
<--- Score

8. What problems are you facing and how do you consider Release Management will circumvent those obstacles?
<--- Score

9. Who had the original idea?
<--- Score

10. What vendors make products that address the Release Management needs?
<--- Score

11. Will Release Management deliverables need to be tested and, if so, by whom?
<--- Score

12. Is it clear when you think of the day ahead of you

what activities and tasks you need to complete?
<--- Score

13. How does it fit into your organizational needs and tasks?
<--- Score

14. Who else hopes to benefit from it?
<--- Score

15. Does your organization need more Release Management education?
<--- Score

16. How do you assess your Release Management workforce capability and capacity needs, including skills, competencies, and staffing levels?
<--- Score

17. What does Release Management success mean to the stakeholders?
<--- Score

18. What are the timeframes required to resolve each of the issues/problems?
<--- Score

19. What Tools are Needed?
<--- Score

20. Can management personnel recognize the monetary benefit of Release Management?
<--- Score

21. Are problem definition and motivation clearly presented?

<--- Score

22. What are the minority interests and what amount of minority interests can be recognized?
<--- Score

23. What situation(s) led to this Release Management Self Assessment?
<--- Score

24. Which is the sequence of events in choosing a technology tool?
<--- Score

25. What is the smallest subset of the problem you can usefully solve?
<--- Score

26. For your Release Management project, identify and describe the business environment, is there more than one layer to the business environment?
<--- Score

27. Will new equipment/products be required to facilitate Release Management delivery, for example is new software needed?
<--- Score

28. Are you dealing with any of the same issues today as yesterday? What can you do about this?
<--- Score

29. Do you have/need 24-hour access to key personnel?
<--- Score

30. How do you take a forward-looking perspective in identifying Release Management research related to market response and models?
<--- Score

31. Who defines the rules in relation to any given issue?
<--- Score

32. What do you need to start doing?
<--- Score

33. Will it solve real problems?
<--- Score

34. Who are your key stakeholders who need to sign off?
<--- Score

35. What should be considered when identifying available resources, constraints, and deadlines?
<--- Score

36. How are the Release Management's objectives aligned to the organization's overall business strategy?
<--- Score

37. Are controls defined to recognize and contain problems?
<--- Score

38. Looking at each person individually – does every one have the qualities which are needed to work in this group?
<--- Score

39. How do you identify the kinds of information that you will need?
<--- Score

40. What extra resources will you need?
<--- Score

41. Think about the people you identified for your Release Management project and the project responsibilities you would assign to them. what kind of training do you think they would need to perform these responsibilities effectively?
<--- Score

42. How much are sponsors, customers, partners, stakeholders involved in Release Management? In other words, what are the risks, if Release Management does not deliver successfully?
<--- Score

43. Consider your own Release Management project, what types of organizational problems do you think might be causing or affecting your problem, based on the work done so far?
<--- Score

44. Are there Release Management problems defined?
<--- Score

45. Release Unit and Identification is defined
<--- Score

46. As a sponsor, customer or management, how important is it to meet goals, objectives?
<--- Score

47. What are the expected benefits of Release Management to the business?
<--- Score

48. What are the business objectives to be achieved with Release Management?
<--- Score

49. Who needs to know about Release Management?
<--- Score

50. To what extent would your organization benefit from being recognized as a award recipient?
<--- Score

51. What tools and technologies are needed for a custom Release Management project?
<--- Score

52. Are your goals realistic? Do you need to redefine your problem? Perhaps the problem has changed or maybe you have reached your goal and need to set a new one?
<--- Score

53. How are you going to measure success?
<--- Score

54. What else needs to be measured?
<--- Score

55. Should you invest in industry-recognized qualications?
<--- Score

56. Are employees recognized or rewarded for performance that demonstrates the highest levels of integrity?
<--- Score

57. Are there any revenue recognition issues?
<--- Score

58. What are your needs in relation to Release Management skills, labor, equipment, and markets?
<--- Score

59. Are there any specific expectations or concerns about the Release Management team, Release Management itself?
<--- Score

60. When a Release Management manager recognizes a problem, what options are available?
<--- Score

61. Escalation who do operations call in case of a problem?
<--- Score

62. What would happen if Release Management weren't done?
<--- Score

63. Why has no os tool emerged to meet this need?
<--- Score

64. Is the need for organizational change recognized?
<--- Score

65. What prevents you from making the changes

you know will make you a more effective Release Management leader?
<--- Score

66. Have you identified your Release Management key performance indicators?
<--- Score

67. Do you need different information or graphics?
<--- Score

68. What is the problem or issue?
<--- Score

69. What information do users need?
<--- Score

70. What needs to be done?
<--- Score

71. Are you able to pro-actively identify any changes in the behavior of the system?
<--- Score

72. To what extent does each concerned units management team recognize Release Management as an effective investment?
<--- Score

73. Does training need to be revisited before continuing?
<--- Score

74. Do you need to avoid or amend any Release Management activities?
<--- Score

75. When does it need doing?
<--- Score

76. What training and capacity building actions are needed to implement proposed reforms?
<--- Score

Add up total points for this section:
_____ = Total points for this section

Divided by: ______ (number of statements answered) = ______ Average score for this section

Transfer your score to the Release Management Index at the beginning of the Self-Assessment.

CRITERION #2: DEFINE:

INTENT: Formulate the business problem. Define the problem, needs and objectives.

In my belief, the answer to this question is clearly defined:

5 Strongly Agree

4 Agree

3 Neutral

2 Disagree

1 Strongly Disagree

1. Does the current environment support the business and functional requirements?
<--- Score

2. Is Release Management required?
<--- Score

3. As the workload increases, how much additional hardware etc. is required?

<--- Score

4. Are customer(s) identified and segmented according to their different needs and requirements?
<--- Score

5. How was the 'as is' process map developed, reviewed, verified and validated?
<--- Score

6. Has a high-level 'as is' process map been completed, verified and validated?
<--- Score

7. What are the record-keeping requirements of Release Management activities?
<--- Score

8. How did the Release Management manager receive input to the development of a Release Management improvement plan and the estimated completion dates/times of each activity?
<--- Score

9. What are the rough order estimates on cost savings/ opportunities that Release Management brings?
<--- Score

10. A release policy is clearly defined
<--- Score

11. Has a project plan, Gantt chart, or similar been developed/completed?
<--- Score

12. Is the scope of Release Management defined?

<--- Score

13. How will the Release Management team and the organization measure complete success of Release Management?
<--- Score

14. What are the Roles and Responsibilities for each team member and its leadership? Where is this documented?
<--- Score

15. What happens if Release Management's scope changes?
<--- Score

16. Is training required?
<--- Score

17. How do you hand over Release Management context?
<--- Score

18. Required Metrics Defined?
<--- Score

19. Has anyone else (internal or external to the organization) attempted to solve this problem or a similar one before? If so, what knowledge can be leveraged from these previous efforts?
<--- Score

20. When is the estimated completion date?
<--- Score

21. Will the product of the project fail to satisfy

customer requirements if the change request is not executed?
<--- Score

22. Has the improvement team collected the 'voice of the customer' (obtained feedback – qualitative and quantitative)?
<--- Score

23. Do the build instructions include all required components?
<--- Score

24. What are the dynamics of the communication plan?
<--- Score

25. Is the current 'as is' process being followed? If not, what are the discrepancies?
<--- Score

26. Has your scope been defined?
<--- Score

27. In what way can you redefine the criteria of choice clients have in your category in your favor?
<--- Score

28. The Release packaging and Build roles are defined
<--- Score

29. Where do requirements come from (and what should we do about it)?
<--- Score

30. When are meeting minutes sent out? Who is on the distribution list?
<--- Score

31. Is there a critical path to deliver Release Management results?
<--- Score

32. Has a team charter been developed and communicated?
<--- Score

33. Has the Release Management work been fairly and/or equitably divided and delegated among team members who are qualified and capable to perform the work? Has everyone contributed?
<--- Score

34. What sources do you use to gather information for a Release Management study?
<--- Score

35. What is the scope of Release Management?
<--- Score

36. Scope of sensitive information?
<--- Score

37. Who is gathering Release Management information?
<--- Score

38. What are the compelling business reasons for embarking on Release Management?
<--- Score

39. What scope to assess?
<--- Score

40. Is scope creep really all bad news?
<--- Score

41. How does the Release Management manager ensure against scope creep?
<--- Score

42. All CSI activities fall under the scope of Change, Release and Deployment Management
<--- Score

43. What scope do you want your strategy to cover?
<--- Score

44. Has the direction changed at all during the course of Release Management? If so, when did it change and why?
<--- Score

45. What do others require?
<--- Score

46. Is the Release Management scope manageable?
<--- Score

47. Have specific policy objectives been defined?
<--- Score

48. Does the team have regular meetings?
<--- Score

49. Is there a completed SIPOC representation, describing the Suppliers, Inputs, Process, Outputs, and

Customers?
<--- Score

50. If substitutes have been appointed, have they been briefed on the Release Management goals and received regular communications as to the progress to date?
<--- Score

51. Is it clearly defined in and to your organization what you do?
<--- Score

52. Do the problem and goal statements meet the SMART criteria (specific, measurable, attainable, relevant, and time-bound)?
<--- Score

53. Are team charters developed?
<--- Score

54. Is the team sponsored by a champion or business leader?
<--- Score

55. Is the Release Management scope complete and appropriately sized?
<--- Score

56. How do you think the partners involved in Release Management would have defined success?
<--- Score

57. Is Release Management linked to key business goals and objectives?
<--- Score

58. What is the definition of success?
<--- Score

59. How and when will the baselines be defined?
<--- Score

60. When was the Release Management start date?
<--- Score

61. What is the scope of the Release Management effort?
<--- Score

62. How do you manage scope?
<--- Score

63. What platform is required for a particular version?
<--- Score

64. When is the install required by?
<--- Score

65. Is Release Management currently on schedule according to the plan?
<--- Score

66. Is the team formed and are team leaders (Coaches and Management Leads) assigned?
<--- Score

67. Has/have the customer(s) been identified?
<--- Score

68. Are accountability and ownership for Release

Management clearly defined?
<--- Score

69. How do you keep key subject matter experts in the loop?
<--- Score

70. Is there regularly 100% attendance at the team meetings? If not, have appointed substitutes attended to preserve cross-functionality and full representation?
<--- Score

71. Are approval levels defined for contracts and supplements to contracts?
<--- Score

72. Will team members perform Release Management work when assigned and in a timely fashion?
<--- Score

73. Is the improvement team aware of the different versions of a process: what they think it is vs. what it actually is vs. what it should be vs. what it could be?
<--- Score

74. Is there a Release Management management charter, including business case, problem and goal statements, scope, milestones, roles and responsibilities, communication plan?
<--- Score

75. Can be adapted to possible future requirements?
<--- Score

76. Are customers identified and high impact areas defined?
<--- Score

77. What constraints exist that might impact the team?
<--- Score

78. Are there any constraints known that bear on the ability to perform Release Management work? How is the team addressing them?
<--- Score

79. How can the value of Release Management be defined?
<--- Score

80. Where do open source requirements come from (and what should you do about it)?
<--- Score

81. What is in scope?
<--- Score

82. Is full participation by members in regularly held team meetings guaranteed?
<--- Score

83. Has everyone on the team, including the team leaders, been properly trained?
<--- Score

84. The scope for Release and deployment is defined
<--- Score

85. What key business process output measure(s) does Release Management leverage and how?
<--- Score

86. What specifically is the problem? Where does it occur? When does it occur? What is its extent?
<--- Score

87. What defines best in class?
<--- Score

88. Are different versions of process maps needed to account for the different types of inputs?
<--- Score

89. How would you define Release Management leadership?
<--- Score

90. What are the boundaries of the scope? What is in bounds and what is not? What is the start point? What is the stop point?
<--- Score

91. What is the scope?
<--- Score

92. Who are the Release Management improvement team members, including Management Leads and Coaches?
<--- Score

93. What is in the scope and what is not in scope?
<--- Score

94. Have all basic functions of Release Management

been defined?
<--- Score

95. Are roles and responsibilities formally defined?
<--- Score

96. What RESOURCES are required to deliver the change?
<--- Score

97. What are the tasks and definitions?
<--- Score

98. What would be the goal or target for a Release Management's improvement team?
<--- Score

99. Who defines (or who defined) the rules and roles?
<--- Score

100. How do you gather Release Management requirements?
<--- Score

101. Are required metrics defined, what are they?
<--- Score

102. Is data collected and displayed to better understand customer(s) critical needs and requirements.
<--- Score

103. Is the team adequately staffed with the desired cross-functionality? If not, what additional resources are available to the team?
<--- Score

104. What system do you use for gathering Release Management information?
<--- Score

105. Have the customer needs been translated into specific, measurable requirements? How?
<--- Score

106. How will variation in the actual durations of each activity be dealt with to ensure that the expected Release Management results are met?
<--- Score

107. Why are you doing Release Management and what is the scope?
<--- Score

108. What was the context?
<--- Score

109. What critical content must be communicated – who, what, when, where, and how?
<--- Score

110. Is the team equipped with available and reliable resources?
<--- Score

111. Do you all define Release Management in the same way?
<--- Score

112. Will team members regularly document their Release Management work?
<--- Score

113. What customer feedback methods were used to solicit their input?
<--- Score

114. Are improvement team members fully trained on Release Management?
<--- Score

115. Is a fully trained team formed, supported, and committed to work on the Release Management improvements?
<--- Score

116. Are task requirements clearly defined?
<--- Score

117. Have all of the relationships been defined properly?
<--- Score

118. How often are the team meetings?
<--- Score

119. What Release Management requirements should be gathered?
<--- Score

120. Does the scope remain the same?
<--- Score

121. Are resources adequate for the scope?
<--- Score

122. What is out of scope?
<--- Score

123. Is there a completed, verified, and validated high-level 'as is' (not 'should be' or 'could be') business process map?
<--- Score

124. Are business processes mapped?
<--- Score

125. How is the team tracking and documenting its work?
<--- Score

126. What baselines are required to be defined and managed?
<--- Score

127. Are there different segments of customers?
<--- Score

128. Is Service Delivery (hardware/software/ people) capable of supporting requirements?
<--- Score

129. What is the context?
<--- Score

130. Are audit criteria, scope, frequency and methods defined?
<--- Score

131. What is the RETURN required from the change?
<--- Score

132. What is out-of-scope initially?

<--- Score

133. Release and deployment models are defined
<--- Score

134. How would you define the culture at your organization, how susceptible is it to Release Management changes?
<--- Score

135. The release and deployment roles are defined
<--- Score

Add up total points for this section:
_____ = Total points for this section

Divided by: ______ (number of statements answered) = ______ Average score for this section

Transfer your score to the Release Management Index at the beginning of the Self-Assessment.

CRITERION #3: MEASURE:

INTENT: Gather the correct data. Measure the current performance and evolution of the situation.

In my belief, the answer to this question is clearly defined:

5 Strongly Agree

4 Agree

3 Neutral

2 Disagree

1 Strongly Disagree

1. What key measures identified indicate the performance of the business process?
<--- Score

2. Is there a systematic policy of technology upgrade, to ensure that costly systems are decommissioned when new ones are deployed?
<--- Score

3. Does Release Management analysis show the relationships among important Release Management factors?
<--- Score

4. Why do you expend time and effort to implement measurement, for whom?
<--- Score

5. How do you aggregate measures across priorities?
<--- Score

6. The approach of traditional Release Management works for detail complexity but is focused on a systematic approach rather than an understanding of the nature of systems themselves, what approach will permit your organization to deal with the kind of unpredictable emergent behaviors that dynamic complexity can introduce?
<--- Score

7. What is the right balance of time and resources between investigation, analysis, and discussion and dissemination?
<--- Score

8. What are the agreed upon definitions of the high impact areas, defect(s), unit(s), and opportunities that will figure into the process capability metrics?
<--- Score

9. Have you found any 'ground fruit' or 'low-hanging fruit' for immediate remedies to the gap in performance?
<--- Score

10. What causes investor action?
<--- Score

11. What would be a real cause for concern?
<--- Score

12. What are the types and number of measures to use?
<--- Score

13. How much do political issues impact on the decision in open source projects and how does this ultimately impact on innovation?
<--- Score

14. Are process variation components displayed/ communicated using suitable charts, graphs, plots?
<--- Score

15. Is data collected on key measures that were identified?
<--- Score

16. Has the appropriate access to relevant data and analysis capability been granted?
<--- Score

17. Have the concerns of stakeholders to help identify and define potential barriers been obtained and analyzed?
<--- Score

18. Are missed Release Management opportunities costing your organization money?
<--- Score

19. Cost of downtime due to bad code last year?
<--- Score

20. What causes extra work or rework?
<--- Score

21. What measurements are being captured?
<--- Score

22. When should sunk cost be abandoned and new solutions sought ?
<--- Score

23. What are your key Release Management indicators that you will measure, analyze and track?
<--- Score

24. Who participated in the data collection for measurements?
<--- Score

25. How do you measure variability?
<--- Score

26. Did you tackle the cause or the symptom?
<--- Score

27. Are high impact defects defined and identified in the business process?
<--- Score

28. Was a data collection plan established?
<--- Score

29. Can you measure the return on analysis?
<--- Score

30. Which stakeholder characteristics are analyzed?
<--- Score

31. How do you unambiguously measure success?
<--- Score

32. Will Release Management have an impact on current business continuity, disaster recovery processes and/or infrastructure?
<--- Score

33. Do staff have the necessary skills to collect, analyze, and report data?
<--- Score

34. How do you control the overall costs of your work processes?
<--- Score

35. Is key measure data collection planned and executed, process variation displayed and communicated and performance baselined?
<--- Score

36. Are there measurements based on task performance?
<--- Score

37. Verify business objectives. Are they appropriate, and well-articulated?
<--- Score

38. What measurements are possible, practicable and meaningful?
<--- Score

39. What are your key Release Management organizational performance measures, including key short and longer-term financial measures?
<--- Score

40. What relevant entities could be measured?
<--- Score

41. Is it possible to estimate the impact of unanticipated complexity such as wrong or failed assumptions, feedback, etc. on proposed reforms?
<--- Score

42. What harm might be caused?
<--- Score

43. Are losses documented, analyzed, and remedial processes developed to prevent future losses?
<--- Score

44. How is the value delivered by Release Management being measured?
<--- Score

45. What is measured? Why?
<--- Score

46. What could cause you to change course?
<--- Score

47. What causes mismanagement?
<--- Score

48. How will your organization measure success?
<--- Score

49. How do you identify and analyze stakeholders and their interests?
<--- Score

50. How do you stay flexible and focused to recognize larger Release Management results?
<--- Score

51. Are you taking your company in the direction of better and revenue or cheaper and cost?
<--- Score

52. What causes innovation to fail or succeed in your organization?
<--- Score

53. How do you do risk analysis of rare, cascading, catastrophic events?
<--- Score

54. Does your organization systematically track and analyze outcomes related for accountability and quality improvement?
<--- Score

55. Are key measures identified and agreed upon?
<--- Score

56. How do you focus on what is right -not who is right?
<--- Score

57. What is the total cost related to deploying Release Management, including any consulting or professional services?

<--- Score

58. Is Process Variation Displayed/Communicated?
<--- Score

59. Does the Release Management task fit the client's priorities?
<--- Score

60. What data was collected (past, present, future/ ongoing)?
<--- Score

61. What are the uncertainties surrounding estimates of impact?
<--- Score

62. What particular quality tools did the team find helpful in establishing measurements?
<--- Score

63. What methods are feasible and acceptable to estimate the impact of reforms?
<--- Score

64. Why do the measurements/indicators matter?
<--- Score

65. Is there a Performance Baseline?
<--- Score

66. Should a more thorough impact analysis be conducted?
<--- Score

67. Do you aggressively reward and promote the

people who have the biggest impact on creating excellent Release Management services/products?
<--- Score

68. Have all non-recommended alternatives been analyzed in sufficient detail?
<--- Score

69. Have you made assumptions about the shape of the future, particularly its impact on your customers and competitors?
<--- Score

70. Can you do Release Management without complex (expensive) analysis?
<--- Score

71. What does Release Management cost?
<--- Score

72. Does Release Management systematically track and analyze outcomes for accountability and quality improvement?
<--- Score

73. What disadvantage does this cause for the user?
<--- Score

74. Pressured to cut change-related costs?
<--- Score

75. Is the solution cost-effective?
<--- Score

76. How is performance measured?
<--- Score

77. How do you measure success?
<--- Score

78. How will you measure your Release Management effectiveness?
<--- Score

79. Are there any easy-to-implement alternatives to Release Management? Sometimes other solutions are available that do not require the cost implications of a full-blown project?
<--- Score

80. Are the units of measure consistent?
<--- Score

81. Have changes been properly/adequately analyzed for effect?
<--- Score

82. How can you measure the performance?
<--- Score

83. Where is it measured?
<--- Score

84. What potential environmental factors impact the Release Management effort?
<--- Score

85. How will measures be used to manage and adapt?
<--- Score

86. Are you aware of what could cause a problem?
<--- Score

87. Are the measurements objective?
<--- Score

88. How frequently do you track Release Management measures?
<--- Score

89. Is long term and short term variability accounted for?
<--- Score

90. What are the costs of reform?
<--- Score

91. How can you measure Release Management in a systematic way?
<--- Score

92. What charts has the team used to display the components of variation in the process?
<--- Score

93. Should there be some prioritization to fixes?
<--- Score

94. Is a solid data collection plan established that includes measurement systems analysis?
<--- Score

95. What has the team done to assure the stability and accuracy of the measurement process?
<--- Score

96. What are your customers expectations and measures?

<--- Score

97. Do you effectively measure and reward individual and team performance?
<--- Score

98. What are the key input variables? What are the key process variables? What are the key output variables?
<--- Score

99. Among the Release Management product and service cost to be estimated, which is considered hardest to estimate?
<--- Score

100. How do you know that any Release Management analysis is complete and comprehensive?
<--- Score

101. Which measures and indicators matter?
<--- Score

102. Is data collection planned and executed?
<--- Score

103. How do you measure lifecycle phases?
<--- Score

104. What is an unallowable cost?
<--- Score

105. How do you measure efficient delivery of Release Management services?
<--- Score

106. What are the costs associated?

<--- Score

107. Have the types of risks that may impact Release Management been identified and analyzed?
<--- Score

108. How do your measurements capture actionable Release Management information for use in exceeding your customers expectations and securing your customers engagement?
<--- Score

109. How is progress measured?
<--- Score

110. How will success or failure be measured?
<--- Score

111. What do you measure and why?
<--- Score

112. How to cause the change?
<--- Score

113. What evidence is there and what is measured?
<--- Score

114. How will effects be measured?
<--- Score

115. Does Release Management analysis isolate the fundamental causes of problems?
<--- Score

116. How will you measure success?
<--- Score

117. How are measurements made?
<--- Score

118. How large is the gap between current performance and the customer-specified (goal) performance?
<--- Score

119. Who should receive measurement reports?
<--- Score

120. Able to be supported at a reasonable cost?
<--- Score

121. What could cause delays in the schedule?
<--- Score

Add up total points for this section:
_____ = Total points for this section

Divided by: ______ (number of statements answered) = ______ Average score for this section

Transfer your score to the Release Management Index at the beginning of the Self-Assessment.

CRITERION #4: ANALYZE:

INTENT: Analyze causes, assumptions and hypotheses.

In my belief, the answer to this question is clearly defined:

5 Strongly Agree

4 Agree

3 Neutral

2 Disagree

1 Strongly Disagree

1. Are gaps between current performance and the goal performance identified?
<--- Score

2. How do you identify specific Release Management investment opportunities and emerging trends?
<--- Score

3. How do you promote understanding that opportunity for improvement is not criticism of the

status quo, or the people who created the status quo?
<--- Score

4. What does the data say about the performance of the business process?
<--- Score

5. Do your leaders quickly bounce back from setbacks?
<--- Score

6. Process support: how can a project better institutionalize workflow support without adding a bureaucratic burden to the developers?
<--- Score

7. How do you measure the operational performance of your key work systems and processes, including productivity, cycle time, and other appropriate measures of process effectiveness, efficiency, and innovation?
<--- Score

8. Is the Release Management process severely broken such that a re-design is necessary?
<--- Score

9. What data is gathered?
<--- Score

10. Where is Release Management data gathered?
<--- Score

11. Are the changes were recorded so that the author of the change and what others changed is logged in a database so that, if needed, the change

can be reset to its original value?
<--- Score

12. Were Pareto charts (or similar) used to portray the 'heavy hitters' (or key sources of variation)?
<--- Score

13. What were the crucial 'moments of truth' on the process map?
<--- Score

14. Is Data and process analysis, root cause analysis and quantifying the gap/opportunity in place?
<--- Score

15. What tools were used to generate the list of possible causes?
<--- Score

16. What controls do you have in place to protect data?
<--- Score

17. What successful thing are you doing today that may be blinding you to new growth opportunities?
<--- Score

18. What are your current levels and trends in key Release Management measures or indicators of product and process performance that are important to and directly serve your customers?
<--- Score

19. When conducting a business process reengineering study, what do you look for when trying to identify business processes to change?

<--- Score

20. What are the disruptive Release Management technologies that enable your organization to radically change your business processes?
<--- Score

21. What other organizational variables, such as reward systems or communication systems, affect the performance of this Release Management process?
<--- Score

22. Do several people in different organizational units assist with the Release Management process?
<--- Score

23. To what extent is OS ideology implicated in the process of tool choice and development, or is it rather invoked to justify positions based on other factors?
<--- Score

24. What is your organizations process which leads to recognition of value generation?
<--- Score

25. Can you add value to the current Release Management decision-making process (largely qualitative) by incorporating uncertainty modeling (more quantitative)?
<--- Score

26. What are the revised rough estimates of the financial savings/opportunity for Release Management improvements?
<--- Score

27. Did any value-added analysis or 'lean thinking' take place to identify some of the gaps shown on the 'as is' process map?
<--- Score

28. How do you implement and manage your work processes to ensure that they meet design requirements?
<--- Score

29. What tools were used to narrow the list of possible causes?
<--- Score

30. Is the suppliers process defined and controlled?
<--- Score

31. Is the required Release Management data gathered?
<--- Score

32. Able to recover quickly from a failure of one or more components of the overall system?
<--- Score

33. How do you use Release Management data and information to support organizational decision making and innovation?
<--- Score

34. Have any additional benefits been identified that will result from closing all or most of the gaps?
<--- Score

35. What is the cost of poor quality as supported by

the team's analysis?
<--- Score

36. How often will data be collected for measures?
<--- Score

37. Are Release Management changes recognized early enough to be approved through the regular process?
<--- Score

38. Build and Release tools (that provide listings of input and output CIs) are in place
<--- Score

39. Was everyone informed of the new process?
<--- Score

40. What are the best opportunities for value improvement?
<--- Score

41. An organizationally feasible system request is one that considers the mission, goals and objectives of the organization. Key questions are: is the Release Management solution request practical and will it solve a problem or take advantage of an opportunity to achieve company goals?
<--- Score

42. What Processes are currently specified and used?
<--- Score

43. What conclusions were drawn from the team's data collection and analysis? How did the team reach

these conclusions?
<--- Score

44. What are your Release Management processes?
<--- Score

45. What process should you select for improvement?
<--- Score

46. What are your key performance measures or indicators and in-process measures for the control and improvement of your Release Management processes?
<--- Score

47. Was a detailed process map created to amplify critical steps of the 'as is' business process?
<--- Score

48. Is it possible to get a quality product out of this design process?
<--- Score

49. What did the team gain from developing a sub-process map?
<--- Score

50. How is the way you as the leader think and process information affecting your organizational culture?
<--- Score

51. What methods do you use to gather Release Management data?
<--- Score

52. Is the gap/opportunity displayed and

communicated in financial terms?
<--- Score

53. What is the level of your satisfaction with the project management structures, processes, and personnel?
<--- Score

54. What Release Management data do you gather or use now?
<--- Score

55. Are data file references within components correct?
<--- Score

56. Are all data files available?
<--- Score

57. Think about some of the processes you undertake within your organization, which do you own?
<--- Score

58. Identify an operational issue in your organization. for example, could a particular task be done more quickly or more efficiently by Release Management?
<--- Score

59. How does the organization define, manage, and improve its Release Management processes?
<--- Score

60. What are your best practices for minimizing Release Management project risk, while demonstrating incremental value and quick wins throughout the Release Management project

lifecycle?
<--- Score

61. Do your employees have the opportunity to do what they do best everyday?
<--- Score

62. Is the performance gap determined?
<--- Score

63. Do your contracts/agreements contain data security obligations?
<--- Score

64. What other jobs or tasks affect the performance of the steps in the Release Management process?
<--- Score

65. What processes are in place for engaging with other technical teams to consider emerging technologies?
<--- Score

66. What quality tools were used to get through the analyze phase?
<--- Score

67. Were any designed experiments used to generate additional insight into the data analysis?
<--- Score

68. What are your current levels and trends in key measures or indicators of Release Management product and process performance that are important to and directly serve your customers? How do these results compare with the performance of your

competitors and other organizations with similar offerings?
<--- Score

69. Record-keeping requirements flow from the records needed as inputs, outputs, controls and for transformation of a Release Management process. Are the records needed as inputs to the Release Management process available?
<--- Score

70. How do the existing processes and procedures facilitate the day-to-day running of IT Production, and its relationship with the Business Sponsors and IT Development ?
<--- Score

71. How was the detailed process map generated, verified, and validated?
<--- Score

72. How do your work systems and key work processes relate to and capitalize on your core competencies?
<--- Score

73. Have the problem and goal statements been updated to reflect the additional knowledge gained from the analyze phase?
<--- Score

74. Were there any improvement opportunities identified from the process analysis?
<--- Score

75. A compounding model resolution with available

relevant data can often provide insight towards a solution methodology; which Release Management models, tools and techniques are necessary?
<--- Score

76. Was a cause-and-effect diagram used to explore the different types of causes (or sources of variation)?
<--- Score

77. How do mission and objectives affect the Release Management processes of your organization?
<--- Score

78. Where is the data coming from to measure compliance?
<--- Score

79. The purpose, goal and objective of the Release and Deployment Management process is defined
<--- Score

80. Do you, as a leader, bounce back quickly from setbacks?
<--- Score

81. Think about the functions involved in your Release Management project, what processes flow from these functions?
<--- Score

82. What were the financial benefits resulting from any 'ground fruit or low-hanging fruit' (quick fixes)?
<--- Score

83. Is the process able to run unattended for long periods of time without intervention?

<--- Score

84. Did any additional data need to be collected?
<--- Score

85. How is Release Management data gathered?
<--- Score

Add up total points for this section:
_____ = Total points for this section

Divided by: ______ (number of statements answered) = ______ Average score for this section

Transfer your score to the Release Management Index at the beginning of the Self-Assessment.

CRITERION #5: IMPROVE:

INTENT: Develop a practical solution. Innovate, establish and test the solution and to measure the results.

In my belief, the answer to this question is clearly defined:

5 Strongly Agree

4 Agree

3 Neutral

2 Disagree

1 Strongly Disagree

1. Does it avoid poorly executed software handoffs between development, testing, and operations?
<--- Score

2. Are there any constraints (technical, political, cultural, or otherwise) that would inhibit certain solutions?
<--- Score

3. How do you define the solutions' scope?
<--- Score

4. How do you decide how much to remunerate an employee?
<--- Score

5. Every design decision is technical, or not?
<--- Score

6. Do you combine technical expertise with business knowledge and Release Management Key topics include lifecycles, development approaches, requirements and how to make a business case?
<--- Score

7. How significant is the improvement in the eyes of the end user?
<--- Score

8. Are the best solutions selected?
<--- Score

9. What tools were used to tap into the creativity and encourage 'outside the box' thinking?
<--- Score

10. How will you know that you have improved?
<--- Score

11. Improve the production readiness and quality of your application code?
<--- Score

12. What are the implications of the one critical Release Management decision 10 minutes, 10

months, and 10 years from now?
<--- Score

13. Were any criteria developed to assist the team in testing and evaluating potential solutions?
<--- Score

14. What are your current levels and trends in key measures or indicators of workforce and leader development?
<--- Score

15. Are you assessing Release Management and risk?
<--- Score

16. Risk(s) associated with the change. What could go wrong by carrying out the change?
<--- Score

17. What is, really, the difference between development and innovation, i.e. how big or radical do changes have to be to warrant the label 'innovation' ?
<--- Score

18. What tools do you use once you have decided on a Release Management strategy and more importantly how do you choose?
<--- Score

19. What actually has to improve and by how much?
<--- Score

20. Is there a cost/benefit analysis of optimal solution(s)?
<--- Score

21. Is the requested change request a result of changes in other project(s)?
<--- Score

22. How do the Release Management results compare with the performance of your competitors and other organizations with similar offerings?
<--- Score

23. Is the solution technically practical?
<--- Score

24. When was the first version of your solution released?
<--- Score

25. For estimation problems, how do you develop an estimation statement?
<--- Score

26. How will you know when its improved?
<--- Score

27. How will the organization know that the solution worked?
<--- Score

28. How do you measure progress and evaluate training effectiveness?
<--- Score

29. Did everyone understand what was required of them?
<--- Score

30. What attendant changes will need to be made to ensure that the solution is successful?
<--- Score

31. What tools were used to evaluate the potential solutions?
<--- Score

32. Risk events: what are the things that could go wrong?
<--- Score

33. What can you do to improve?
<--- Score

34. Is a contingency plan established?
<--- Score

35. Do those selected for the Release Management team have a good general understanding of what Release Management is all about?
<--- Score

36. To what extent does management recognize Release Management as a tool to increase the results?
<--- Score

37. Why improve in the first place?
<--- Score

38. What should a proof of concept or pilot accomplish?
<--- Score

39. Risk factors: what are the characteristics of Release Management that make it risky?

<--- Score

40. In the past few months, what is the smallest change you have made that has had the biggest positive result? What was it about that small change that produced the large return?
<--- Score

41. In some projects up to 85% of the changes are performed by a small core of developers, what space for innovation is left?
<--- Score

42. How do you improve your likelihood of success ?
<--- Score

43. How do you link measurement and risk?
<--- Score

44. What tools were most useful during the improve phase?
<--- Score

45. How do you measure risk?
<--- Score

46. How well are os projects documented?
<--- Score

47. How can you improve Release Management?
<--- Score

48. How do you manage and improve your Release Management work systems to deliver customer value and achieve organizational success and sustainability?
<--- Score

49. What happens after development: how should developers release component-based software and how can users subsequently obtain such software— especially if the software under consideration consists of many components that are released by many organizations at many different geographical locations?
<--- Score

50. What is the magnitude of the improvements?
<--- Score

51. Are risk triggers captured?
<--- Score

52. What is the team's contingency plan for potential problems occurring in implementation?
<--- Score

53. Is user documentation available?
<--- Score

54. Is the measure of success for Release Management understandable to a variety of people?
<--- Score

55. What is the risk?
<--- Score

56. Risk Identification: What are the possible risk events your organization faces in relation to Release Management?
<--- Score

57. How do you avoid poorly executed software

handoffs between development, testing, and operations?
<--- Score

58. Deliver results consistently & repeat ably, irrespective of changed circumstances ?
<--- Score

59. Is the scope clearly documented?
<--- Score

60. How does the team improve its work?
<--- Score

61. At what point will vulnerability assessments be performed once Release Management is put into production (e.g., ongoing Risk Management after implementation)?
<--- Score

62. Does the goal represent a desired result that can be measured?
<--- Score

63. What do you want to improve?
<--- Score

64. How risky is your organization?
<--- Score

65. What error proofing will be done to address some of the discrepancies observed in the 'as is' process?
<--- Score

66. Who controls key decisions that will be made?
<--- Score

67. Does it Improve the production readiness and quality of your application code?
<--- Score

68. Was a pilot designed for the proposed solution(s)?
<--- Score

69. What aspects of the Deliver model should be improved or extended?
<--- Score

70. How will the team or the process owner(s) monitor the implementation plan to see that it is working as intended?
<--- Score

71. What went well, what should change, what can improve?
<--- Score

72. Is supporting Release Management documentation required?
<--- Score

73. If you could go back in time five years, what decision would you make differently? What is your best guess as to what decision you're making today you might regret five years from now?
<--- Score

74. Is pilot data collected and analyzed?
<--- Score

75. Do you cover the five essential competencies: Communication, Collaboration,Innovation,

Adaptability, and Leadership that improve an organization's ability to leverage the new Release Management in a volatile global economy?
<--- Score

76. Is open source software development faster, better, and cheaper than software engineering?
<--- Score

77. What does the 'should be' process map/design look like?
<--- Score

78. How do you improve Release Management service perception, and satisfaction?
<--- Score

79. What is the implementation plan?
<--- Score

80. What is the Release Management's sustainability risk?
<--- Score

81. What communications are necessary to support the implementation of the solution?
<--- Score

82. Are new and improved process ('should be') maps developed?
<--- Score

83. What to do with the results or outcomes of measurements?
<--- Score

84. What improvements have been achieved?
<--- Score

85. What are the development, release, and deployment activities?
<--- Score

86. What were the underlying assumptions on the cost-benefit analysis?
<--- Score

87. How did the team generate the list of possible solutions?
<--- Score

88. What lessons, if any, from a pilot were incorporated into the design of the full-scale solution?
<--- Score

89. Is a solution implementation plan established, including schedule/work breakdown structure, resources, risk management plan, cost/budget, and control plan?
<--- Score

90. Who are the people involved in developing and implementing Release Management?
<--- Score

91. How do you keep improving Release Management?
<--- Score

92. Are the Users / Customers content with the result?
<--- Score

93. How do developers concur over long distances in environments where people rarely if ever meet face to face in a virtual organization?
<--- Score

94. What is Release Management's impact on utilizing the best solution(s)?
<--- Score

95. For decision problems, how do you develop a decision statement?
<--- Score

96. How will you measure the results?
<--- Score

97. Is there a small-scale pilot for proposed improvement(s)? What conclusions were drawn from the outcomes of a pilot?
<--- Score

98. What are the issues that arise when a limited number of vendors participate in a technology market and how can the risks be mitigated ?
<--- Score

99. How are you helping customers benefit from the capabilities in the next release of a solution?
<--- Score

100. Are improved process ('should be') maps modified based on pilot data and analysis?
<--- Score

101. How can you improve performance?

<--- Score

102. How do you measure improved Release Management service perception, and satisfaction?
<--- Score

103. How can skill-level changes improve Release Management?
<--- Score

104. Describe the design of the pilot and what tests were conducted, if any?
<--- Score

105. How do you go about comparing Release Management approaches/solutions?
<--- Score

106. What resources are required for the improvement efforts?
<--- Score

107. Who will be responsible for documenting the Release Management requirements in detail?
<--- Score

108. How do you improve the production readiness and quality of your application code?
<--- Score

109. How do you improve productivity?
<--- Score

110. Is there a high likelihood that any recommendations will achieve their intended results?
<--- Score

111. Have all required components been placed under control during development?
<--- Score

112. Can you identify any significant risks or exposures to Release Management third- parties (vendors, service providers, alliance partners etc) that concern you?
<--- Score

113. Which of the recognised risks out of all risks can be most likely transferred?
<--- Score

114. How will you know that a change is an improvement?
<--- Score

115. Is open source software development essentially an agile method?
<--- Score

116. Who controls the risk?
<--- Score

117. Explorations of the frontiers of Release Management will help you build influence, improve Release Management, optimize decision making, and sustain change, what is your approach?
<--- Score

118. Are possible solutions generated and tested?
<--- Score

119. Who will be using the results of the measurement

activities?
<--- Score

120. Is the implementation plan designed?
<--- Score

121. What needs improvement? Why?
<--- Score

122. How does the solution remove the key sources of issues discovered in the analyze phase?
<--- Score

123. Will the controls trigger any other risks?
<--- Score

124. Is the optimal solution selected based on testing and analysis?
<--- Score

125. Have you identified breakpoints and/or risk tolerances that will trigger broad consideration of a potential need for intervention or modification of strategy?
<--- Score

126. Information/context awareness: how can a developer/participant restore awareness in project activity after having been offline for a few hours, days, or weeks?
<--- Score

127. Can the solution be designed and implemented within an acceptable time period?
<--- Score

128. Who will be responsible for making the decisions to include or exclude requested changes once Release Management is underway?
<--- Score

129. Which solutions are on a release management cycle?
<--- Score

130. Is a solution production-ready?
<--- Score

131. What practices helps your organization to develop its capacity to recognize patterns?
<--- Score

Add up total points for this section:
_____ = Total points for this section

Divided by: ______ (number of statements answered) = ______ Average score for this section

Transfer your score to the Release Management Index at the beginning of the Self-Assessment.

CRITERION #6: CONTROL:

INTENT: Implement the practical solution. Maintain the performance and correct possible complications.

In my belief, the answer to this question is clearly defined:

5 Strongly Agree

4 Agree

3 Neutral

2 Disagree

1 Strongly Disagree

1. Does Release Management appropriately measure and monitor risk?
<--- Score

2. Is knowledge gained on process shared and institutionalized?
<--- Score

3. Who will be in control?

<--- Score

4. Do you monitor the effectiveness of your Release Management activities?
<--- Score

5. Does the response plan contain a definite closed loop continual improvement scheme (e.g., plan-do-check-act)?
<--- Score

6. Did the Regression Plan work correctly?
<--- Score

7. Did the Implementation plan work correctly/as planned?
<--- Score

8. What are the key elements of your Release Management performance improvement system, including your evaluation, organizational learning, and innovation processes?
<--- Score

9. Are pertinent alerts monitored, analyzed and distributed to appropriate personnel?
<--- Score

10. Is new knowledge gained imbedded in the response plan?
<--- Score

11. Monitoring required?
<--- Score

12. How will report readings be checked to effectively

monitor performance?
<--- Score

13. Who sets the Release Management standards?
<--- Score

14. How is change control managed?
<--- Score

15. How do your controls stack up?
<--- Score

16. What do your reports reflect?
<--- Score

17. Where do ideas that reach policy makers and planners as proposals for Release Management strengthening and reform actually originate?
<--- Score

18. What are you attempting to measure/monitor?
<--- Score

19. Who is the Release Management process owner?
<--- Score

20. How will input, process, and output variables be checked to detect for sub-optimal conditions?
<--- Score

21. How might the organization capture best practices and lessons learned so as to leverage improvements across the business?
<--- Score

22. What are your results for key measures or

indicators of the accomplishment of your Release Management strategy and action plans, including building and strengthening core competencies?
<--- Score

23. Does a troubleshooting guide exist or is it needed?
<--- Score

24. Has the improved process and its steps been standardized?
<--- Score

25. How do you establish and deploy modified action plans if circumstances require a shift in plans and rapid execution of new plans?
<--- Score

26. How do controls support value?
<--- Score

27. Will existing staff require re-training, for example, to learn new business processes?
<--- Score

28. What other areas of the organization might benefit from the Release Management team's improvements, knowledge, and learning?
<--- Score

29. How can you best use all of your knowledge repositories to enhance learning and sharing?
<--- Score

30. Implementation Planning: is a pilot needed to test the changes before a full roll out occurs?
<--- Score

31. What is the recommended frequency of auditing?
<--- Score

32. Is there a Release Management Communication plan covering who needs to get what information when?
<--- Score

33. Is there a standardized process?
<--- Score

34. What key inputs and outputs are being measured on an ongoing basis?
<--- Score

35. Who controls critical resources?
<--- Score

36. Do the attributes of the configuration object reflect the change?
<--- Score

37. What is the best design framework for Release Management organization now that, in a post industrial-age if the top-down, command and control model is no longer relevant?
<--- Score

38. Will your goals reflect your program budget?
<--- Score

39. How will you measure your QA plan's effectiveness?
<--- Score

40. Has the post-production plan been established?
<--- Score

41. What is the control/monitoring plan?
<--- Score

42. What are the critical parameters to watch?
<--- Score

43. How do senior leaders actions reflect a commitment to the organizations Release Management values?
<--- Score

44. Was the software process followed and software engineering standards applied?
<--- Score

45. When do you start to place an entity under configuration control?
<--- Score

46. In the case of a Release Management project, the criteria for the audit derive from implementation objectives. an audit of a Release Management project involves assessing whether the recommendations outlined for implementation have been met. Can you track that any Release Management project is implemented as planned, and is it working?
<--- Score

47. How do you select, collect, align, and integrate Release Management data and information for tracking daily operations and overall organizational performance, including progress relative to strategic

objectives and action plans?
<--- Score

48. Are the planned controls working?
<--- Score

49. Can support from partners be adjusted?
<--- Score

50. What is your theory of human motivation, and how does your compensation plan fit with that view?
<--- Score

51. Have all components been backed up and a recovery plan been defined?
<--- Score

52. We have a policy for planning release and deployment packages
<--- Score

53. Will any special training be provided for results interpretation?
<--- Score

54. Are controls in place and consistently applied?
<--- Score

55. What do you measure to verify effectiveness gains?
<--- Score

56. Are the planned controls in place?
<--- Score

57. How easy is it to amend or adjust the

configuration of the application, and its environmental behavior?
<--- Score

58. What can you control?
<--- Score

59. Is reporting being used or needed?
<--- Score

60. What should the next improvement project be that is related to Release Management?
<--- Score

61. Will the team be available to assist members in planning investigations?
<--- Score

62. Was the Regression Plan needed?
<--- Score

63. What should you measure to verify efficiency gains?
<--- Score

64. Can you adapt and adjust to changing Release Management situations?
<--- Score

65. Does the Release Management performance meet the customer's requirements?
<--- Score

66. Who has control over resources?
<--- Score

67. Are there technical standards within IT Production against which developers should develop solutions?
<--- Score

68. How do you encourage people to take control and responsibility?
<--- Score

69. Is there a menu of standard technologies that developers must adhere to?
<--- Score

70. How do you create standards?
<--- Score

71. Are suggested corrective/restorative actions indicated on the response plan for known causes to problems that might surface?
<--- Score

72. Is a response plan established and deployed?
<--- Score

73. Are operating procedures consistent?
<--- Score

74. Is there documentation that will support the successful operation of the improvement?
<--- Score

75. When is a release management plan used?
<--- Score

76. You may have created your quality measures at a time when you lacked resources, technology wasn't

up to the required standard, or low service levels were the industry norm. Have those circumstances changed?
<--- Score

77. Notifications: Have all impacted parties been notified about the Release Plan and schedule?
<--- Score

78. Is there a control plan in place for sustaining improvements (short and long-term)?
<--- Score

79. The planning of releases is managed
<--- Score

80. How will new or emerging customer needs/ requirements be checked/communicated to orient the process toward meeting the new specifications and continually reducing variation?
<--- Score

81. Are there documented procedures?
<--- Score

82. Is a response plan in place for when the input, process, or output measures indicate an 'out-of-control' condition?
<--- Score

83. Are new process steps, standards, and documentation ingrained into normal operations?
<--- Score

84. Have new or revised work instructions resulted?
<--- Score

85. Are you measuring, monitoring and predicting Release Management activities to optimize operations and profitability, and enhancing outcomes?
<--- Score

86. Act/Adjust: What Do you Need to Do Differently?
<--- Score

87. Were the resources required to implement the Change as planned?
<--- Score

88. What other systems, operations, processes, and infrastructures (hiring practices, staffing, training, incentives/rewards, metrics/dashboards/scorecards, etc.) need updates, additions, changes, or deletions in order to facilitate knowledge transfer and improvements?
<--- Score

89. How will the process owner verify improvement in present and future sigma levels, process capabilities?
<--- Score

90. What do you stand for--and what are you against?
<--- Score

91. Is there a recommended audit plan for routine surveillance inspections of Release Management's gains?
<--- Score

92. Who must complete a release management plan?
<--- Score

93. How likely is the current Release Management plan to come in on schedule or on budget?
<--- Score

94. Is the Technology based on general Open Standards?
<--- Score

95. What adjustments to the strategies are needed?
<--- Score

96. How are such Standards updated?
<--- Score

97. Do the Release Management decisions you make today help people and the planet tomorrow?
<--- Score

98. How do you plan on providing proper recognition and disclosure of supporting companies?
<--- Score

99. Is there a transfer of ownership and knowledge to process owner and process team tasked with the responsibilities.
<--- Score

100. Against what alternative is success being measured?
<--- Score

101. How will the process owner and team be able to hold the gains?
<--- Score

102. What quality tools were useful in the control phase?
<--- Score

103. What are the known security controls?
<--- Score

104. Is there a documented and implemented monitoring plan?
<--- Score

105. Are documented procedures clear and easy to follow for the operators?
<--- Score

106. Does job training on the documented procedures need to be part of the process team's education and training?
<--- Score

107. Do you monitor the Release Management decisions made and fine tune them as they evolve?
<--- Score

108. How will the day-to-day responsibilities for monitoring and continual improvement be transferred from the improvement team to the process owner?
<--- Score

Add up total points for this section:
_____ = Total points for this section

Divided by: ______ (number of statements answered) = ______
Average score for this section

Transfer your score to the Release Management Index at the beginning of the Self-Assessment.

CRITERION #7: SUSTAIN:

INTENT: Retain the benefits.

In my belief, the answer to this question is clearly defined:

5 Strongly Agree

4 Agree

3 Neutral

2 Disagree

1 Strongly Disagree

1. What does In Production mean?
<--- Score

2. Deliver interim releases?
<--- Score

3. Have new benefits been realized?
<--- Score

4. Who do we want your customers to become?
<--- Score

5. What did you miss in the interview for the worst hire you ever made?
<--- Score

6. What should you stop doing?
<--- Score

7. Are the criteria for selecting recommendations stated?
<--- Score

8. What is the main reason for establishing a Baseline?
<--- Score

9. Is the appropriate component version specified?
<--- Score

10. What management system can you use to leverage the Release Management experience, ideas, and concerns of the people closest to the work to be done?
<--- Score

11. Eliminate lengthy email threads trying to achieve change approval?
<--- Score

12. Who is responsible for ensuring appropriate resources (time, people and money) are allocated to Release Management?
<--- Score

13. Which functions and people interact with the supplier and or customer?

<--- Score

14. What one word do you want to own in the minds of your customers, employees, and partners?
<--- Score

15. Have all interfaces been tested?
<--- Score

16. Can you break it down?
<--- Score

17. A Service Owner is responsible for which ?
<--- Score

18. Who will determine interim and final deadlines?
<--- Score

19. How can you negotiate Release Management successfully with a stubborn boss, an irate client, or a deceitful coworker?
<--- Score

20. Who do you want your customers to become?
<--- Score

21. What versions are affected by component X changes?
<--- Score

22. To whom do you add value?
<--- Score

23. How much does Release Management help?
<--- Score

24. How do you govern and fulfill your societal responsibilities?
<--- Score

25. What is a feasible sequencing of reform initiatives over time?
<--- Score

26. How are changes managed?
<--- Score

27. Reduce your release window by 90%?
<--- Score

28. What theoretical and methodological tools are available to us as researchers to study such aspects of Release Management?
<--- Score

29. Who has a particular system version?
<--- Score

30. How do you know if you are successful?
<--- Score

31. Can you do all this work?
<--- Score

32. What relationships among Release Management trends do you perceive?
<--- Score

33. How do you provide a safe environment -physically and emotionally?
<--- Score

34. Is the right version of the compiler and other software tools specified?
<--- Score

35. What could go wrong?
<--- Score

36. Which selection of CIs should be managed?
<--- Score

37. What are strategies for increasing support and reducing opposition?
<--- Score

38. What are your most important goals for the strategic Release Management objectives?
<--- Score

39. Do you have the necessary Technology experience?
<--- Score

40. What happens if you do not have enough funding?
<--- Score

41. What versions are affected by a change to component X?
<--- Score

42. Who is responsible for Release Management?
<--- Score

43. If you find that you havent accomplished one of the goals for one of the steps of the Release Management strategy, what will you do to fix it?

<--- Score

44. Who does it?
<--- Score

45. How do you track customer value, profitability or financial return, organizational success, and sustainability?
<--- Score

46. What are the rules and assumptions your industry operates under? What if the opposite were true?
<--- Score

47. Who has a particular software version?
<--- Score

48. How do we know that all tasks are complete?
<--- Score

49. Is Release Management realistic, or are you setting yourself up for failure?
<--- Score

50. What is your competitive advantage?
<--- Score

51. What have you done to protect your business from competitive encroachment?
<--- Score

52. Is Release Management dependent on the successful delivery of a current project?
<--- Score

53. Were all related SCIs properly updated?

<--- Score

54. What is it like to work for you?
<--- Score

55. Is the impact that Release Management has shown?
<--- Score

56. Were those responsible for installing hardware and software aware of the existence of the build procedure?
<--- Score

57. In retrospect, of the projects that you pulled the plug on, what percent do you wish had been allowed to keep going, and what percent do you wish had ended earlier?
<--- Score

58. If you had to rebuild your organization without any traditional competitive advantages (i.e., no killer a technology, promising research, innovative product/service delivery model, etc.), how would your people have to approach their work and collaborate together in order to create the necessary conditions for success?
<--- Score

59. Is it economical; do you have the time and money?
<--- Score

60. What is the recommended frequency of auditing?
<--- Score

61. What is the craziest thing you can do?

<--- Score

62. Are you satisfied with your current role? If not, what is missing from it?
<--- Score

63. Whose voice (department, ethnic group, women, older workers, etc) might you have missed hearing from in your company, and how might you amplify this voice to create positive momentum for your business?
<--- Score

64. Who is on the team?
<--- Score

65. Who is RESPONSIBLE for the build, test and implementation of the change?
<--- Score

66. Who is responsible for what?
<--- Score

67. How do you foster the skills, knowledge, talents, attributes, and characteristics you want to have?
<--- Score

68. Has an FTR been conducted to assess technical correctness?
<--- Score

69. How do you set Release Management stretch targets and how do you get people to not only participate in setting these stretch targets but also that they strive to achieve these?
<--- Score

70. Why use Release Management?
<--- Score

71. Is system being built for the right platform?
<--- Score

72. What are current Release Management paradigms?
<--- Score

73. Which models, tools and techniques are necessary?
<--- Score

74. Why will customers want to buy your organizations products/services?
<--- Score

75. How long will the install take?
<--- Score

76. How likely is it that a customer would recommend your company to a friend or colleague?
<--- Score

77. Is the Technology Safe and Sound?
<--- Score

78. How do you maintain Release Management's Integrity?
<--- Score

79. Change and release scheduling is an integrated activity of change management
<--- Score

80. Do you feel that more should be done in the Release Management area?
<--- Score

81. How can models be created and managed to support the expression of design intent not directly manifest in code?
<--- Score

82. Are assumptions made in Release Management stated explicitly?
<--- Score

83. Are you relevant? Will you be relevant five years from now? Ten?
<--- Score

84. What Release Management skills are most important?
<--- Score

85. How long will it take to change?
<--- Score

86. Can you handle the increased load expected in 6 months?
<--- Score

87. What are the essentials of internal Release Management management?
<--- Score

88. Is the appropriate version specified for each build component?
<--- Score

89. What was the last experiment you ran?
<--- Score

90. Who are four people whose careers you have enhanced?
<--- Score

91. Who will be responsible for deciding whether Release Management goes ahead or not after the initial investigations?
<--- Score

92. Who is the beneficiary?
<--- Score

93. Are there any activities that you can take off your to do list?
<--- Score

94. How do you deal with Release Management changes?
<--- Score

95. What are the challenges?
<--- Score

96. Has all formal testing been completed including unit, integration, and system tests?
<--- Score

97. Release design options are considered
<--- Score

98. Have training materials been completed for Operations, Support and end-users?

<--- Score

99. What counts that you are not counting?
<--- Score

100. Ask what perspective would this service address?
<--- Score

101. Who will provide the final approval of Release Management deliverables?
<--- Score

102. How many reported faults for version Y?
<--- Score

103. How do you create buy-in?
<--- Score

104. Do you have the right people on the bus?
<--- Score

105. Why is it important to have senior management support for a Release Management project?
<--- Score

106. What projects are going on in the organization today, and what resources are those projects using from the resource pools?
<--- Score

107. Did your employees make progress today?
<--- Score

108. Do you see more potential in people than they do in themselves?

<--- Score

109. Are you maintaining a past–present–future perspective throughout the Release Management discussion?
<--- Score

110. How do you engage the workforce, in addition to satisfying them?
<--- Score

111. Instead of going to current contacts for new ideas, what if you reconnected with dormant contacts--the people you used to know? If you were going reactivate a dormant tie, who would it be?
<--- Score

112. Have you eliminated lengthy email threads trying to achieve change approval?
<--- Score

113. What unique value proposition (UVP) do you offer?
<--- Score

114. Are you changing as fast as the world around you?
<--- Score

115. Ask yourself: Is the product sellable, shippable, supportable and scaleable?
<--- Score

116. How important is Release Management to the user organizations mission?
<--- Score

117. Do you think you know, or do you know you know ?
<--- Score

118. Is there a budget?
<--- Score

119. Who do you think the world wants your organization to be?
<--- Score

120. Who are your customers?
<--- Score

121. How do you determine the key elements that affect Release Management workforce satisfaction, how are these elements determined for different workforce groups and segments?
<--- Score

122. Do you say no to customers for no reason?
<--- Score

123. How do customers see your organization?
<--- Score

124. Who is it for?
<--- Score

125. What can a cms do for an open source project?
<--- Score

126. What is effective Release Management?
<--- Score

127. What are the potential basics of Release Management fraud?
<--- Score

128. Why do and why don't your customers like your organization?
<--- Score

129. Are new benefits received and understood?
<--- Score

130. Have there been any unexpected/undesirable side effects?
<--- Score

131. What trophy do you want on your mantle?
<--- Score

132. How do you assess the Release Management pitfalls that are inherent in implementing it?
<--- Score

133. How easy is it to find help?
<--- Score

134. Does it Eliminate lengthy email threads trying to achieve change approval?
<--- Score

135. How can you become more high-tech but still be high touch?
<--- Score

136. Where do changes come from?
<--- Score

137. What is your BATNA (best alternative to a negotiated agreement)?
<--- Score

138. What happens when a new employee joins the organization?
<--- Score

139. What is something you believe that nearly no one agrees with you on?
<--- Score

140. What goals did you miss?
<--- Score

141. Are Users authenticated and Authorized, and non-users Isolated?
<--- Score

142. If no one would ever find out about your accomplishments, how would you lead differently?
<--- Score

143. What are the key enablers to make this Release Management move?
<--- Score

144. Political -is anyone trying to undermine this project?
<--- Score

145. What are the short and long-term Release Management goals?
<--- Score

146. What modeling instruments are available?

<--- Score

147. Who uses Release Management?
<--- Score

148. Have both the Customer and the Service Owner agreed to the terms of the SLA?
<--- Score

149. What is the overall talent health of your organization as a whole at senior levels, and for each organization reporting to a member of the Senior Leadership Team?
<--- Score

150. Who, on the executive team or the board, has spoken to a customer recently?
<--- Score

151. What would have to be true for the option on the table to be the best possible choice?
<--- Score

152. What may be the consequences for the performance of an organization if all stakeholders are not consulted regarding Release Management?
<--- Score

153. Operational - will it work?
<--- Score

154. What is the RELATIONSHIP between this change and other changes?
<--- Score

155. Do you have the right capabilities and capacities?

<--- Score

156. How many Authorizations for Release of Information forms are being submitted with an application?
<--- Score

157. Where can you break convention?
<--- Score

158. Are manual updates allowed?
<--- Score

159. Who will manage the integration of tools?
<--- Score

160. What trouble can you get into?
<--- Score

161. Which individuals, teams or departments will be involved in Release Management?
<--- Score

162. How do you listen to customers to obtain actionable information?
<--- Score

163. Does Agile Release Management Work in Real Life?
<--- Score

164. Are the assumptions believable and achievable?
<--- Score

165. In the past year, what have you done (or could you have done) to increase the accurate perception of

your company/brand as ethical and honest?
<--- Score

166. How do you make it meaningful in connecting Release Management with what users do day-to-day?
<--- Score

167. How much time is spent waiting/wasted?
<--- Score

168. How are you doing compared to your industry?
<--- Score

169. What is the overall business strategy?
<--- Score

170. What current systems have to be understood and/or changed?
<--- Score

171. What is the kind of project structure that would be appropriate for your Release Management project, should it be formal and complex, or can it be less formal and relatively simple?
<--- Score

172. Able to respond to the failure of all components of the system?
<--- Score

173. When Release Management for new application services is or will be integrated with your ITSM capabilities. How is it integrated?
<--- Score

174. What are you trying to prove to yourself, and how

might it be hijacking your life and business success?
<--- Score

175. How will you ensure you get what you expected?
<--- Score

176. How do you manage Release Management Knowledge Management (KM)?
<--- Score

177. Do you know what you are doing? And who do you call if you don't?
<--- Score

178. What is being changed and why?
<--- Score

179. When Does Release Management Apply to Project Management?
<--- Score

180. What will drive Release Management change?
<--- Score

181. Does everyone who should know how to access software?
<--- Score

182. Do Release Management rules make a reasonable demand on a users capabilities?
<--- Score

183. What business benefits will Release Management goals deliver if achieved?
<--- Score

184. Were lessons learned captured and communicated?
<--- Score

185. What is the REASON for the change?
<--- Score

186. What would you recommend your friend do if he/she were facing this dilemma?
<--- Score

187. How do you stay inspired?
<--- Score

188. What are the gaps in your knowledge and experience?
<--- Score

189. How do you ensure that implementations of Release Management products are done in a way that ensures safety?
<--- Score

190. Ask yourself: how would you do this work if you only had one staff member to do it?
<--- Score

191. What are you challenging?
<--- Score

192. How often are new product releases anticipated?
<--- Score

193. What are the success criteria that will indicate that Release Management objectives have been met

and the benefits delivered?
<--- Score

194. When information truly is ubiquitous, when reach and connectivity are completely global, when computing resources are infinite, and when a whole new set of impossibilities are not only possible, but happening, what will that do to your business?
<--- Score

195. What information is critical to your organization that your executives are ignoring?
<--- Score

196. What are the usability implications of Release Management actions?
<--- Score

197. What you are going to do to affect the numbers?
<--- Score

198. Are your responses positive or negative?
<--- Score

199. What happens if the typical user behavior changes?
<--- Score

200. What is release management?
<--- Score

201. Will there be any necessary staff changes (redundancies or new hires)?
<--- Score

202. Who have you, as a company, historically been

when you've been at your best?
<--- Score

203. What are internal and external Release Management relations?
<--- Score

204. What threat is Release Management addressing?
<--- Score

205. What is the purpose of Release Management in relation to the mission?
<--- Score

206. Spending too much time deploying changes in a virtualized environment?
<--- Score

207. How do you transition from the baseline to the target?
<--- Score

208. How do senior leaders deploy your organizations vision and values through your leadership system, to the workforce, to key suppliers and partners, and to customers and other stakeholders, as appropriate?
<--- Score

209. How will you insure seamless interoperability of Release Management moving forward?
<--- Score

210. When was change implemented?
<--- Score

211. Was the Change implemented on time?

<--- Score

212. What do we do when new problems arise?
<--- Score

213. Will the project fail if the change request is not executed?
<--- Score

214. How do you foster innovation?
<--- Score

215. Will it be accepted by users?
<--- Score

216. What potential megatrends could make your business model obsolete?
<--- Score

217. Has the change specified been made without modifications?
<--- Score

218. Why should you adopt a Release Management framework?
<--- Score

219. What is your formula for success in Release Management ?
<--- Score

220. If your customer were your grandmother, would you tell her to buy what you're selling?
<--- Score

221. Does the suggested change request

represent a desired enhancement to the products functionality?
<--- Score

222. What happens at your organization when people fail?
<--- Score

223. What technologies form the basis of the legacy system?
<--- Score

224. What will be the consequences to the stakeholder (financial, reputation etc) if Release Management does not go ahead or fails to deliver the objectives?
<--- Score

225. How will you know that the Release Management project has been successful?
<--- Score

226. If you got fired and a new hire took your place, what would she do different?
<--- Score

227. Who has a stake in the outcomes?
<--- Score

228. In a project to restructure Release Management outcomes, which stakeholders would you involve?
<--- Score

229. How do you accomplish your long range Release Management goals?
<--- Score

230. Has implementation been effective in reaching specified objectives so far?
<--- Score

231. What have been your experiences in defining long range Release Management goals?
<--- Score

232. How do you know it has worked?
<--- Score

233. Is the Release Management organization completing tasks effectively and efficiently?
<--- Score

234. What is the source of the strategies for Release Management strengthening and reform?
<--- Score

235. What is the estimated value of the project?
<--- Score

236. How will you motivate the stakeholders with the least vested interest?
<--- Score

237. What knowledge, skills and characteristics mark a good Release Management project manager?
<--- Score

238. How does Release Management work?
<--- Score

239. How will software changes affect system performance?

<--- Score

240. Able to restore the system to a known state at a specific period of time?
<--- Score

241. Have all walkthroughs, peer reviews, and management reviews been performed throughout the project?
<--- Score

242. What to build, how to build it, build it, and is it built right?
<--- Score

243. How are the release blocks to be managed?
<--- Score

244. Was the build procedure template easy to follow and complete?
<--- Score

245. How do you proactively clarify deliverables and Release Management quality expectations?
<--- Score

246. What do we know about proximity and distance in work groups?
<--- Score

247. Is there a work around that you can use?
<--- Score

248. If you had to leave your organization for a year and the only communication you could have with employees/colleagues was a single paragraph, what

would you write?
<--- Score

249. How do you keep the momentum going?
<--- Score

250. Is there any existing Release Management governance structure?
<--- Score

251. What are the business goals Release Management is aiming to achieve?
<--- Score

252. How can you become the company that would put you out of business?
<--- Score

253. Think of your Release Management project, what are the main functions?
<--- Score

254. Do you have an implicit bias for capital investments over people investments?
<--- Score

255. Release and deployment technology tools are in place
<--- Score

256. Are there any disadvantages to implementing Release Management? There might be some that are less obvious?
<--- Score

257. What is an unauthorized commitment?

<--- Score

258. If you do not follow, then how to lead?
<--- Score

259. Can you Reduce your release window by 90%?
<--- Score

260. At what moment would you think; Will I get fired?
<--- Score

261. When you map the key players in your own work and the types/domains of relationships with them, which relationships do you find easy and which challenging, and why?
<--- Score

262. Are there any guarantees that the project will ever be completed?
<--- Score

263. What tools and techniques are use to support these activities?
<--- Score

264. Do you think Release Management accomplishes the goals you expect it to accomplish?
<--- Score

265. What must you excel at?
<--- Score

266. Who made the change?
<--- Score

267. Who is the main stakeholder, with ultimate

responsibility for driving Release Management forward?
<--- Score

268. Has the Change had the desired effect & met its objectives?
<--- Score

269. How can you incorporate support to ensure safe and effective use of Release Management into the services that you provide?
<--- Score

270. How do you go about securing Release Management?
<--- Score

271. What Tools are in place?
<--- Score

272. If there were zero limitations, what would you do differently?
<--- Score

273. What could go wrong by carrying out the change?
<--- Score

274. How do you keep records, of what?
<--- Score

275. What does downtime mean to you?
<--- Score

276. What is your Release Management strategy?
<--- Score

277. All tasks complete?
<--- Score

278. Who are the key stakeholders?
<--- Score

279. How does Release Management integrate with other business initiatives?
<--- Score

280. Why should you contact the IT PMO?
<--- Score

281. How is implementation research currently incorporated into each of your goals?
<--- Score

282. Which Release Management goals are the most important?
<--- Score

283. Is there any reason to believe the opposite of my current belief?
<--- Score

284. Better, and cheaper than software engineering?
<--- Score

285. What kind of crime could a potential new hire have committed that would not only not disqualify him/her from being hired by your organization, but would actually indicate that he/she might be a particularly good fit?
<--- Score

286. What are specific Release Management rules to follow?
<--- Score

287. Which component should you upgrade next?
<--- Score

288. Is the correct versions of the compiler and other tools specified?
<--- Score

289. Has training been scheduled for support staff, operations, and the client?
<--- Score

290. If you were responsible for initiating and implementing major changes in your organization, what steps might you take to ensure acceptance of those changes?
<--- Score

291. Is a Release Management team work effort in place?
<--- Score

292. Is your basic point _____ or _____?
<--- Score

293. How much contingency will be available in the budget?
<--- Score

294. What does your signature ensure?
<--- Score

295. Which is a good use of a baseline?
<--- Score

296. Does the number of severity levels matter?
<--- Score

297. What stupid rule would you most like to kill?
<--- Score

298. Are you using a design thinking approach and integrating Innovation, Release Management Experience, and Brand Value?
<--- Score

299. What Release Management modifications can you make work for you?
<--- Score

300. What are the barriers to increased Release Management production?
<--- Score

301. How do you cross-sell and up-sell your Release Management success?
<--- Score

302. Is maximizing Release Management protection the same as minimizing Release Management loss?
<--- Score

303. Does the suggested change request seem to represent a necessary enhancement to the product?
<--- Score

304. What will happen to the software

configuration of a customer, when one updates a certain component?
<--- Score

305. How is the change to be tested?
<--- Score

306. Wasting staff time by performing configuration changes manually?
<--- Score

307. What is the range of capabilities?
<--- Score

308. Why should people listen to you?
<--- Score

309. Are you making progress, and are you making progress as Release Management leaders?
<--- Score

310. Is it possible to regress the Change?
<--- Score

311. What is the role of the Change Advisory Board (CAB)?
<--- Score

312. Marketing budgets are tighter, consumers are more skeptical, and social media has changed forever the way we talk about Release Management. How do you gain traction?
<--- Score

313. What are the regression possibilities if the change is terminated?

<--- Score

314. How is release management for new application services integrated with your ITSM capabilities?
<--- Score

315. Who else should you help?
<--- Score

316. When should technology be recycled & re-used ?
<--- Score

317. Who is responsible for errors?
<--- Score

318. Are you / should you be revolutionary or evolutionary?
<--- Score

319. What are your service levels for fixes, service desk, etc. Will you reduce fees if the service levels are not met?
<--- Score

320. Why is Release Management important for you now?
<--- Score

321. What is the funding source for this project?
<--- Score

322. Have benefits been optimized with all key stakeholders?
<--- Score

323. Would you rather sell to knowledgeable and informed customers or to uninformed customers?
<--- Score

324. Which two other Service Management disciplines does Release Management work with most closely?
<--- Score

325. Can you maintain your growth without detracting from the factors that have contributed to your success?
<--- Score

326. What new services of functionality will be implemented next with Release Management ?
<--- Score

327. Whom among your colleagues do you trust, and for what?
<--- Score

328. How do you lead with Release Management in mind?
<--- Score

329. What are the long-term Release Management goals?
<--- Score

330. Do you have enough freaky customers in your portfolio pushing you to the limit day in and day out?
<--- Score

331. What role does communication play in the

success or failure of a Release Management project?
<--- Score

332. Can the schedule be done in the given time?
<--- Score

333. Are all key stakeholders present at all Structured Walkthroughs?
<--- Score

334. If you weren't already in this business, would you enter it today? And if not, what are you going to do about it?
<--- Score

335. What is your question? Why?
<--- Score

336. What are the top 3 things at the forefront of your Release Management agendas for the next 3 years?
<--- Score

337. How many reported faults in version X?
<--- Score

338. Change Detail – Summary of the change . What is being changed and why?
<--- Score

339. Do you have existing automation or deployment tools?
<--- Score

340. Was the licence list updated?
<--- Score

341. If your company went out of business tomorrow, would anyone who doesn't get a paycheck here care?
<--- Score

342. Who uses your product in ways you never expected?
<--- Score

343. Is your strategy driving your strategy? Or is the way in which you allocate resources driving your strategy?
<--- Score

344. Why not do Release Management?
<--- Score

345. When to buy vs. build ?
<--- Score

346. Are you paying enough attention to the partners your company depends on to succeed?
<--- Score

347. Do you have past Release Management successes?
<--- Score

348. What are your personal philosophies regarding Release Management and how do they influence your work?
<--- Score

Add up total points for this section:
_____ = Total points for this section

Divided by: ______ (number of

statements answered) = ______
Average score for this section

Transfer your score to the Release Management Index at the beginning of the Self-Assessment.

Release Management and Managing Projects, Criteria for Project Managers:

1.0 Initiating Process Group: Release Management

1. Who is involved in each phase?

2. Who supports, improves, and oversees standardized processes related to the Release Management projects program?

3. Who does what?

4. Specific - is the objective clear in terms of what, how, when, and where the situation will be changed?

5. Are you certain deliverables are properly completed and meet quality standards?

6. Are you just doing busywork to pass the time?

7. Mitigate. what will you do to minimize the impact should the risk event occur?

8. Do you know all the stakeholders impacted by the Release Management project and what needs are?

9. How do you help others satisfy needs?

10. How can you make your needs known?

11. Were escalated issues resolved promptly?

12. What will be the pressing issues of tomorrow?

13. The Release Management project managers have maximum authority in which type of organization?

14. What were things that you did very well and want to do the same again on the next Release Management project?

15. Realistic - are the desired results expressed in a way that the team will be motivated and believe that the required level of involvement will be obtained?

16. Where must it be done?

17. If action is called for, what form should it take?

18. What areas does the group agree are the biggest success on the Release Management project?

19. When are the deliverables to be generated in each phase?

20. Do you know the roles & responsibilities required for this Release Management project?

1.1 Project Charter: Release Management

21. What is the business need?

22. When?

23. Customer: who are you doing the Release Management project for?

24. What ideas do you have for initial tests of change (PDSA cycles)?

25. Did your Release Management project ask for this?

26. Why is it important?

27. Avoid costs, improve service, and/ or comply with a mandate?

28. How will you learn more about the process or system you are trying to improve?

29. What are the constraints?

30. Are there special technology requirements?

31. What outcome, in measureable terms, are you hoping to accomplish?

32. Must Have?

33. Why have you chosen the aim you have set forth?

34. How much?

35. Strategic fit: what is the strategic initiative identifier for this Release Management project?

36. What barriers do you predict to your success?

37. How high should you set your goals?

38. How do you manage integration?

39. Environmental stewardship and sustainability considerations: what is the process that will be used to ensure compliance with the environmental stewardship policy?

40. Does the Release Management project need to consider any special capacity or capability issues?

1.2 Stakeholder Register: Release Management

41. What are the major Release Management project milestones requiring communications or providing communications opportunities?

42. What opportunities exist to provide communications?

43. Who wants to talk about Security?

44. How big is the gap?

45. Is your organization ready for change?

46. What is the power of the stakeholder?

47. How much influence do they have on the Release Management project?

48. How will reports be created?

49. What & Why?

50. How should employers make voices heard?

51. Who are the stakeholders?

52. Who is managing stakeholder engagement?

1.3 Stakeholder Analysis Matrix: Release Management

53. Seasonality, weather effects?

54. How do you manage Release Management project Risk?

55. Do recommendations include actions to address any differential distribution of impacts?

56. What can the stakeholder prevent from happening?

57. What is the stakeholders power and status in relation to the Release Management project?

58. Timescales, deadlines and pressures?

59. What is the stakeholders mandate, what is mission?

60. What do you Evaluate?

61. Beneficiaries; who are the potential beneficiaries?

62. Why do you need to manage Release Management project Risk?

63. What resources might the stakeholder bring to the Release Management project?

64. Is there evidence that demonstrates the impact

of education on the Release Management projects outcomes?

65. Market developments?

66. Experience, knowledge, data?

67. How are you predicting what future (work)loads will be?

68. Vital contracts and partners?

69. How are the threatened Release Management project targets being used?

70. How to measure the achievement of the Immediate Objective?

71. Lack of competitive strength?

72. Competitor intentions - various?

2.0 Planning Process Group: Release Management

73. How can you tell when you are done?

74. How many days can task X be late in starting without affecting the Release Management project completion date?

75. How well will the chosen processes produce the expected results?

76. Will the products created live up to the necessary quality?

77. To what extent is the program helping to influence your organizations policy framework?

78. Are there efficient coordination mechanisms to avoid overloading the counterparts, participating stakeholders?

79. Explanation: is what the Release Management project intents to solve a hard question?

80. Have operating capacities been created and/or reinforced in partners?

81. What is the critical path for this Release Management project, and what is the duration of the critical path?

82. Are work methodologies, financial instruments,

etc. shared among departments, organizations and Release Management projects?

83. In what way has the Release Management project come up with innovative measures for problem-solving?

84. What factors are contributing to progress or delay in the achievement of products and results?

85. What do you need to do?

86. What is the NEXT thing to do?

87. What will you do to minimize the impact should a risk event occur?

88. How will you know you did it?

89. Product breakdown structure (pbs): what is the Release Management project result or product, and how should it look like, what are its parts?

90. Have more efficient (sensitive) and appropriate measures been adopted to respond to the political and socio-cultural problems identified?

91. If task x starts two days late, what is the effect on the Release Management project end date?

2.1 Project Management Plan: Release Management

92. Does the implementation plan have an appropriate division of responsibilities?

93. Do the proposed changes from the Release Management project include any significant risks to safety?

94. Why do you manage integration?

95. If the Release Management project management plan is a comprehensive document that guides you in Release Management project execution and control, then what should it NOT contain?

96. What data/reports/tools/etc. do program managers need?

97. Who manages integration?

98. What are the assumptions?

99. What are the training needs?

100. Does the selected plan protect privacy?

101. Are there any windfall benefits that would accrue to the Release Management project sponsor or other parties?

102. Are calculations and results of analyzes

essentially correct?

103. Are the proposed Release Management project purposes different than a previously authorized Release Management project?

104. Is there anything you would now do differently on your Release Management project based on past experience?

105. How can you best help your organization to develop consistent practices in Release Management project management planning stages?

106. Where does all this information come from?

107. What would you do differently what did not work?

108. When is the Release Management project management plan created?

109. What does management expect of PMs?

2.2 Scope Management Plan: Release Management

110. Are the Release Management project team members located locally to the users/stakeholders?

111. Is the Release Management project sponsor clearly communicating the business case or rationale for why this Release Management project is needed?

112. Is the quality assurance team identified?

113. Where do scope processes fit in?

114. Are enough systems & user personnel assigned to the Release Management project?

115. Process groups – where do scope management processes fit in?

116. How do you know how you are doing?

117. Does the Release Management project have a Statement of Work?

118. Are measurements and feedback mechanisms incorporated in tracking work effort & refining work estimating techniques?

119. Why do you need to manage scope?

120. Is the assigned Release Management project manager a PMP (Certified Release Management

project manager) and experienced?

121. Have Release Management project success criteria been defined?

122. When is corrective or preventative action required?

123. Have all documents been archived in a Release Management project repository for each release?

124. How are you planning to maintain the scope baseline and how will you manage scope changes?

125. Has your organization done similar tasks before?

126. What is the unique product, service or result?

127. Have the personnel with the necessary skills and competence been identified and has agreement for participation in the Release Management project been reached with the appropriate management?

128. Pop quiz – which are the same inputs as in scope planning?

2.3 Requirements Management Plan: Release Management

129. Controlling Release Management project requirements involves monitoring the status of the Release Management project requirements and managing changes to the requirements. Who is responsible for monitoring and tracking the Release Management project requirements?

130. Which hardware or software, related to, or as outcome of the Release Management project is new to your organization?

131. Is there formal agreement on who has authority to request a change in requirements?

132. Describe the process for rejecting the Release Management project requirements. Who has the authority to reject Release Management project requirements?

133. Will you document changes to requirements?

134. Will you use an assessment of the Release Management project environment as a tool to discover risk to the requirements process?

135. Did you avoid subjective, flowery or non-specific statements?

136. Did you provide clear and concise specifications?

137. Will the contractors involved take full responsibility?

138. What cost metrics will be used?

139. Why manage requirements?

140. After the requirements are gathered and set forth on the requirements register, theyre little more than a laundry list of items. Some may be duplicates, some might conflict with others and some will be too broad or too vague to understand. Describe how the requirements will be analyzed. Who will perform the analysis?

141. Is requirements work dependent on any other specific Release Management project or non-Release Management project activities (e.g. funding, approvals, procurement)?

142. Subject to change control?

143. Does the Release Management project have a Change Control process?

144. In case of software development; Should you have a test for each code module?

145. How will bidders price evaluations be done, by deliverables, phases, or in a big bang?

146. Have stakeholders been instructed in the Change Control process?

147. How will the information be distributed?

148. What are you counting on?

2.4 Requirements Documentation: Release Management

149. Who is involved?

150. Is your business case still valid?

151. How linear / iterative is your Requirements Gathering process (or will it be)?

152. How can you document system requirements?

153. What are the acceptance criteria?

154. What will be the integration problems?

155. What are the attributes of a customer?

156. What variations exist for a process?

157. What facilities must be supported by the system?

158. Consistency. are there any requirements conflicts?

159. What if the system wasn t implemented?

160. Is the origin of the requirement clearly stated?

161. How will the proposed Release Management project help?

162. How will they be documented / shared?

163. How much testing do you need to do to prove that your system is safe?

164. What is effective documentation?

165. Where are business rules being captured?

166. What kind of entity is a problem ?

167. Is new technology needed?

168. How does what is being described meet the business need?

2.5 Requirements Traceability Matrix: Release Management

169. How do you manage scope?

170. Why use a WBS?

171. What is the WBS?

172. What percentage of Release Management projects are producing traceability matrices between requirements and other work products?

173. Do you have a clear understanding of all subcontracts in place?

174. Is there a requirements traceability process in place?

175. Describe the process for approving requirements so they can be added to the traceability matrix and Release Management project work can be performed. Will the Release Management project requirements become approved in writing?

176. Why do you manage scope?

177. Will you use a Requirements Traceability Matrix?

178. What are the chronologies, contingencies, consequences, criteria?

179. How will it affect the stakeholders personally in

their career?

180. How small is small enough?

2.6 Project Scope Statement: Release Management

181. What are the defined meeting materials?

182. Have the reports to be produced, distributed, and filed been defined?

183. Did your Release Management project ask for this?

184. Are there backup strategies for key members of the Release Management project?

185. What is a process you might recommend to verify the accuracy of the research deliverable?

186. Is this process communicated to the customer and team members?

187. Change management vs. change leadership - what is the difference?

188. What actions will be taken to mitigate the risk?

189. How will you haverify the accuracy of the work of the Release Management project, and what constitutes acceptance of the deliverables?

190. Are the meetings set up to have assigned note takers that will add action/issues to the issue list?

191. Has a method and process for requirement

tracking been developed?

192. Elements that deal with providing the detail?

193. Were potential customers involved early in the planning process?

194. Is an issue management process documented and filed?

195. Are there issues that could affect the existing requirements for the result, service, or product if the scope changes?

196. Any new risks introduced or old risks impacted. Are there issues that could affect the existing requirements for the result, service, or product if the scope changes?

197. Will tasks be marked complete only after QA has been successfully completed?

198. Have you been able to thoroughly document the Release Management projects assumptions and constraints?

199. Is there a process (test plans, inspections, reviews) defined for verifying outputs for each task?

200. Is the plan under configuration management?

2.7 Assumption and Constraint Log: Release Management

201. What strengths do you have?

202. Does the document/deliverable meet general requirements (for example, statement of work) for all deliverables?

203. What other teams / processes would be impacted by changes to the current process, and how?

204. Have all necessary approvals been obtained?

205. Do you know what your customers expectations are regarding this process?

206. Contradictory information between document sections?

207. Have all stakeholders been identified?

208. Is the amount of effort justified by the anticipated value of forming a new process?

209. Does a specific action and/or state that is known to violate security policy occur?

210. How do you design an auditing system?

211. What would you gain if you spent time working to improve this process?

212. Are there procedures in place to effectively manage interdependencies with other Release Management projects / systems?

213. Does a documented Release Management project organizational policy & plan (i.e. governance model) exist?

214. If it is out of compliance, should the process be amended or should the Plan be amended?

215. Is there adequate stakeholder participation for the vetting of requirements definition, changes and management?

216. Is the steering committee active in Release Management project oversight?

217. Are best practices and metrics employed to identify issues, progress, performance, etc.?

218. Model-building: what data-analytic strategies are useful when building proportional-hazards models?

219. Is this model reasonable?

220. Have Release Management project management standards and procedures been established and documented?

2.8 Work Breakdown Structure: Release Management

221. When does it have to be done?

222. Why is it useful?

223. What has to be done?

224. Who has to do it?

225. How much detail?

226. How big is a work-package?

227. Where does it take place?

228. How many levels?

229. How will you and your Release Management project team define the Release Management projects scope and work breakdown structure?

230. Is it still viable?

231. How far down?

232. Can you make it?

233. Is it a change in scope?

234. What is the probability of completing the Release Management project in less that xx days?

235. Why would you develop a Work Breakdown Structure?

236. What is the probability that the Release Management project duration will exceed xx weeks?

237. Do you need another level?

238. When do you stop?

239. Is the work breakdown structure (wbs) defined and is the scope of the Release Management project clear with assigned deliverable owners?

240. When would you develop a Work Breakdown Structure?

2.9 WBS Dictionary: Release Management

241. Are indirect costs accumulated for comparison with the corresponding budgets?

242. Does the contractor have procedures which permit identification of recurring or non-recurring costs as necessary?

243. Is all contract work included in the CWBS?

244. Is the work done on a work package level as described in the WBS dictionary?

245. Are retroactive changes to BCWS and BCWP prohibited except for correction of errors or for normal accounting adjustments?

246. Identify potential or actual overruns and underruns?

247. Can the contractor substantiate work package and planning package budgets?

248. The already stated responsible for overhead performance control of related costs?

249. Is work progressively subdivided into detailed work packages as requirements are defined?

250. Are budgets or values assigned to work packages and planning packages in terms of dollars, hours, or

other measurable units?

251. Authorization to proceed with all authorized work?

252. Time-phased control account budgets?

253. Are significant decision points, constraints, and interfaces identified as key milestones?

254. Are data elements (BCWS, BCWP, and ACWP) progressively summarized from the detail level to the contract level through the CWBS?

255. Are the overhead pools formally and adequately identified?

256. Are meaningful indicators identified for use in measuring the status of cost and schedule performance?

257. Does the contractors system include procedures for measuring the performance of critical subcontractors?

258. Does the contractors system provide for determination of price variance by comparing planned Vs actual commitments?

259. Are the responsibilities and authorities of each of the above organizational elements or managers clearly defined?

2.10 Schedule Management Plan: Release Management

260. How do you manage time?

261. Will rolling way planning be used?

262. Are the constraints or deadlines associated with the task accurate?

263. Sensitivity analysis?

264. Are changes in scope (deliverable commitments) agreed to by all affected groups & individuals?

265. Has the business need been clearly defined?

266. Is there an excessive and invalid use of task constraints and relationships of leads/lags?

267. Has the scope management document been updated and distributed to help prevent scope creep?

268. After initial schedule development, will the schedule be reviewed and validated by the Release Management project team?

269. Are the processes for schedule assessment and analysis defined?

270. Is there a formal process for updating the Release Management project baseline?

271. Is there a Steering Committee in place?

272. Where is the scheduling tool and who has access to it to view it?

273. Have Release Management project team accountabilities & responsibilities been clearly defined?

274. Are internal Release Management project status meetings held at reasonable intervals?

275. Are the results of quality assurance reviews provided to affected groups & individuals?

276. Have Release Management project management standards and procedures been identified / established and documented?

277. Is there a set of procedures defining the scope, procedures, and deliverables defining quality control?

278. Has a provision been made to reassess Release Management project risks at various Release Management project stages?

2.11 Activity List: Release Management

279. What went well?

280. Should you include sub-activities?

281. What went wrong?

282. Are the required resources available or need to be acquired?

283. What is the probability the Release Management project can be completed in xx weeks?

284. How difficult will it be to do specific activities on this Release Management project?

285. Can you determine the activity that must finish, before this activity can start?

286. How will it be performed?

287. What are the critical bottleneck activities?

288. In what sequence?

289. How should ongoing costs be monitored to try to keep the Release Management project within budget?

290. How much slack is available in the Release Management project?

291. How can the Release Management project be displayed graphically to better visualize the activities?

292. Where will it be performed?

293. When will the work be performed?

294. What will be performed?

295. What did not go as well?

296. For other activities, how much delay can be tolerated?

297. What is the LF and LS for each activity?

2.12 Activity Attributes: Release Management

298. What is the general pattern here?

299. Time for overtime?

300. Where else does it apply?

301. What is your organizations history in doing similar activities?

302. Are the required resources available?

303. How difficult will it be to do specific activities on this Release Management project?

304. Does your organization of the data change its meaning?

305. Is there a trend during the year?

306. What conclusions/generalizations can you draw from this?

307. How else could the items be grouped?

308. Have constraints been applied to the start and finish milestones for the phases?

309. Activity: what is Missing?

310. What went right?

311. How many days do you need to complete the work scope with a limit of X number of resources?

312. Activity: fair or not fair?

313. What activity do you think you should spend the most time on?

314. Why?

315. How many resources do you need to complete the work scope within a limit of X number of days?

316. Can you re-assign any activities to another resource to resolve an over-allocation?

2.13 Milestone List: Release Management

317. Who will manage the Release Management project on a day-to-day basis?

318. Can you derive how soon can the whole Release Management project finish?

319. Calculate how long can activity be delayed?

320. How late can each activity be finished and started?

321. Sustainable financial backing?

322. How will you get the word out to customers?

323. How difficult will it be to do specific activities on this Release Management project?

324. Reliability of data, plan predictability?

325. It is to be a narrative text providing the crucial aspects of your Release Management project proposal answering what, who, how, when and where?

326. What has been done so far?

327. Do you foresee any technical risks or developmental challenges?

328. Sustaining internal capabilities?

329. Identify critical paths (one or more) and which activities are on the critical path?

330. What background experience, skills, and strengths does the team bring to your organization?

331. Information and research?

332. Usps (unique selling points)?

333. How will the milestone be verified?

334. How late can the activity finish?

335. Marketing - reach, distribution, awareness?

2.14 Network Diagram: Release Management

336. Where do you schedule uncertainty time?

337. Which type of network diagram allows you to depict four types of dependencies?

338. If a current contract exists, can you provide the vendor name, contract start, and contract expiration date?

339. Planning: who, how long, what to do?

340. What job or jobs precede it?

341. What can be done concurrently?

342. What are the Key Success Factors?

343. What are the tools?

344. What are the Major Administrative Issues?

345. Review the logical flow of the network diagram. Take a look at which activities you have first and then sequence the activities. Do they make sense?

346. What must be completed before an activity can be started?

347. Where do schedules come from?

348. What controls the start and finish of a job?

349. If x is long, what would be the completion time if you break x into two parallel parts of y weeks and z weeks?

350. Are you on time?

351. What to do and When?

352. What is the probability of completing the Release Management project in less that xx days?

353. If the Release Management project network diagram cannot change and you have extra personnel resources, what is the BEST thing to do?

354. What is the completion time?

2.15 Activity Resource Requirements: Release Management

355. How do you handle petty cash?

356. What are constraints that you might find during the Human Resource Planning process?

357. Which logical relationship does the PDM use most often?

358. Do you use tools like decomposition and rolling-wave planning to produce the activity list and other outputs?

359. Why do you do that?

360. Anything else?

361. Other support in specific areas?

362. When does monitoring begin?

363. What is the Work Plan Standard?

364. How many signatures do you require on a check and does this match what is in your policy and procedures?

365. Organizational Applicability?

366. Are there unresolved issues that need to be addressed?

367. Is there anything planned that does not need to be here?

2.16 Resource Breakdown Structure: Release Management

368. Why is this important?

369. Changes based on input from stakeholders?

370. Any changes from stakeholders?

371. Who delivers the information?

372. What is the number one predictor of a groups productivity?

373. How should the information be delivered?

374. What is the difference between % Complete and % work?

375. What is the purpose of assigning and documenting responsibility?

376. The list could probably go on, but, the thing that you would most like to know is, How long & How much?

377. Who is allowed to perform which functions?

378. What can you do to improve productivity?

379. What defines a successful Release Management project?

380. Why do you do it?

381. Is predictive resource analysis being done?

2.17 Activity Duration Estimates: Release Management

382. Calculate the expected duration for an activity that has a most likely time of 3, a pessimistic time of 10, and a optimiztic time of 2?

383. How is the Release Management project doing?

384. Is evaluation criteria defined to rate proposals?

385. If Release Management project time and cost are not as important as the number of resources used each month, which is the BEST thing to do?

386. Do procedures exist describing how the Release Management project scope will be managed?

387. What are crucial elements of successful Release Management project plan execution?

388. Why do you think schedule issues often cause the most conflicts on Release Management projects?

389. Do scope statements include the Release Management project objectives and expected deliverables?

390. Which includes asking team members about the time estimates for activities and reaching agreement on the calendar date for each activity?

391. Is a Release Management project charter created

once a Release Management project is formally recognized?

392. Is risk identification completed regularly throughout the Release Management project?

393. Are measurement techniques employed to determine the potential impact of proposed changes?

394. Does a process exist to determine which risk events to accept and which events to disregard?

395. Why time management?

396. Are contingency plans created to prepare for risk events to occur?

397. Why is activity definition the first process involved in Release Management project time management?

398. Will additional funds be needed for hardware or software?

399. Which type of mathematical analysis is being used?

400. Explanation notice how many choices are half right?

401. Are expert judgment and historical information utilized to estimate activity duration?

2.18 Duration Estimating Worksheet: Release Management

402. When does your organization expect to be able to complete it?

403. When do the individual activities need to start and finish?

404. What is your role?

405. Does the Release Management project provide innovative ways for stakeholders to overcome obstacles or deliver better outcomes?

406. How should ongoing costs be monitored to try to keep the Release Management project within budget?

407. Done before proceeding with this activity or what can be done concurrently?

408. What is the total time required to complete the Release Management project if no delays occur?

409. Can the Release Management project be constructed as planned?

410. What questions do you have?

411. What work will be included in the Release Management project?

412. When, then?

413. What is cost and Release Management project cost management?

414. Small or large Release Management project?

415. Do any colleagues have experience with your organization and/or RFPs?

416. Why estimate costs?

417. What is an Average Release Management project?

2.19 Project Schedule: Release Management

418. Understand the constraints used in preparing the schedule. Are activities connected because logic dictates the order in which others occur?

419. Should you have a test for each code module?

420. Are quality inspections and review activities listed in the Release Management project schedule(s)?

421. How can slack be negative?

422. Did the Release Management project come in under budget?

423. Release Management project work estimates Who is managing the work estimate quality of work tasks in the Release Management project schedule?

424. Why is this particularly bad?

425. Eliminate unnecessary activities. Are there activities that came from a template or previous Release Management project that are not applicable on this phase of this Release Management project?

426. The wbs is developed as part of a joint planning session. and how do you know that youhave done this right?

427. Verify that the update is accurate. Are all

remaining durations correct?

428. How detailed should a Release Management project get?

429. Are all remaining durations correct?

430. Is the Release Management project schedule available for all Release Management project team members to review?

431. Have all Release Management project delays been adequately accounted for, communicated to all stakeholders and adjustments made in overall Release Management project schedule?

432. How do you manage Release Management project Risk?

433. It allows the Release Management project to be delivered on schedule. How Do you Use Schedules?

434. Why is software Release Management project disaster so common?

435. Is the structure for tracking the Release Management project schedule well defined and assigned to a specific individual?

2.20 Cost Management Plan: Release Management

436. Are schedule deliverables actually delivered?

437. Does the Release Management project have a Quality Culture?

438. Contractors scope – how will contractors scope be defined when contracts are let?

439. What is Release Management project management?

440. Is Release Management project work proceeding in accordance with the original Release Management project schedule?

441. Will the forecasts be based on trend analysis and earned value statistics?

442. Forecasts – how will the cost to complete the Release Management project be forecast?

443. Cost estimate preparation – What cost estimates will be prepared during the Release Management project phases?

444. Risk Analysis?

445. Does the schedule include Release Management project management time and change request analysis time?

446. Are the payment terms being followed?

447. Cost / benefit analysis?

448. Are updated Release Management project time & resource estimates reasonable based on the current Release Management project stage?

449. Have all involved Release Management project stakeholders and work groups committed to the Release Management project?

450. Published materials?

451. Are staff skills known and available for each task?

452. Are internal Release Management project status meetings held at reasonable intervals?

453. Are all payments made according to the contract(s)?

454. Are the quality tools and methods identified in the Quality Plan appropriate to the Release Management project?

2.21 Activity Cost Estimates: Release Management

455. Scope statement only direct or indirect costs as well?

456. Was it performed on time?

457. What were things that you did very well and want to do the same again on the next Release Management project?

458. Which contract type places the most risk on the seller?

459. Does the activity serve a common type of customer?

460. What are the audit requirements?

461. Where can you get activity reports?

462. Who determines the quality and expertise of contractors?

463. Who & what determines the need for contracted services?

464. Are data needed on characteristics of care?

465. Were the costs or charges reasonable?

466. What is the activity inventory?

467. What happens if you cannot produce the documentation for the single audit?

468. How do you manage cost?

469. Does the activity use a common approach or business function to deliver its results?

470. Review – what are some common errors in activities to avoid?

471. Measurable - are the targets measurable?

472. What makes a good activity description?

2.22 Cost Estimating Worksheet: Release Management

473. Ask: are others positioned to know, are others credible, and will others cooperate?

474. How will the results be shared and to whom?

475. Is it feasible to establish a control group arrangement?

476. Value pocket identification & quantification what are value pockets?

477. Who is best positioned to know and assist in identifying corresponding factors?

478. Does the Release Management project provide innovative ways for stakeholders to overcome obstacles or deliver better outcomes?

479. What info is needed?

480. What is the estimated labor cost today based upon this information?

481. What will others want?

482. What can be included?

483. Can a trend be established from historical performance data on the selected measure and are the criteria for using trend analysis or forecasting

methods met?

484. What is the purpose of estimating?

485. What costs are to be estimated?

486. Identify the timeframe necessary to monitor progress and collect data to determine how the selected measure has changed?

487. Is the Release Management project responsive to community need?

488. What happens to any remaining funds not used?

489. Will the Release Management project collaborate with the local community and leverage resources?

490. What additional Release Management project(s) could be initiated as a result of this Release Management project?

2.23 Cost Baseline: Release Management

491. Is there anything unique in this Release Management projects scope statement that will affect resources?

492. How difficult will it be to do specific tasks on the Release Management project?

493. Impact to environment?

494. Are you meeting with your team regularly?

495. What does a good WBS NOT look like?

496. How accurate do cost estimates need to be?

497. What can go wrong?

498. Has the Release Management projected annual cost to operate and maintain the product(s) or service(s) been approved and funded?

499. Does it impact schedule, cost, quality?

500. Does the suggested change request represent a desired enhancement to the products functionality?

501. Is there anything you need from upper management in order to be successful?

502. Where do changes come from?

503. Are procedures defined by which the cost baseline may be changed?

504. Does the suggested change request seem to represent a necessary enhancement to the product?

505. For what purpose ?

506. Have the actual milestone completion dates been compared to the approved schedule?

507. How will cost estimates be used?

508. Release Management project goals -should others be reconsidered?

509. How long are you willing to wait before you find out were late?

510. What is cost and Release Management project cost management?

2.24 Quality Management Plan: Release Management

511. How do you manage quality?

512. Where do you focus?

513. How do senior leaders review organizational performance?

514. What are your organizations current levels and trends for the already stated measures related to financial and marketplace performance?

515. What key performance indicators does your organization use to measure, manage, and improve key processes?

516. What data do you gather/use/compile?

517. How do you document and correct nonconformances?

518. Checking the completeness and appropriateness of the sampling and testing. Were the right locations/ samples tested for the right parameters?

519. What is positive about the current process?

520. Were there any deficiencies / issues identified in the prior years self-assessment?

521. Is the steering committee active in Release

Management project oversight?

522. What are your key performance measures/ indicators for tracking progress relative to your action plans?

523. Does the system design reflect the requirements?

524. List your organizations customer contact standards that employees are expected to maintain. How are corresponding standards measured?

525. How does your organization design processes to ensure others meet customer and others requirements?

526. Who gets results of work?

527. How are data handled when a test is not run per specification?

528. What is the Quality Management Plan?

2.25 Quality Metrics: Release Management

529. Is there alignment within your organization on definitions?

530. Is there a set of procedures to capture, analyze and act on quality metrics?

531. Are documents on hand to provide explanations of privacy and confidentiality?

532. Where did complaints, returns and warranty claims come from?

533. What do you measure?

534. How do you know if everyone is trying to improve the right things?

535. When will the Final Guidance will be issued?

536. The metrics–what is being considered?

537. Was the overall quality better or worse than previous products?

538. When is the security analysis testing complete?

539. Which are the right metrics to use?

540. Have alternatives been defined in the event that failure occurs?

541. Are quality metrics defined?

542. Are there already quality metrics available that detect nonlinear embeddings and trends similar to the users perception?

543. What approved evidence based screening tools can be used?

544. What documentation is required?

545. Were quality attributes reported?

546. Is a risk containment plan in place?

547. Has it met internal or external standards?

548. How are requirements conflicts resolved?

2.26 Process Improvement Plan: Release Management

549. Everyone agrees on what process improvement is, right?

550. Have the frequency of collection and the points in the process where measurements will be made been determined?

551. Have storage and access mechanisms and procedures been determined?

552. What makes people good SPI coaches?

553. What is the return on investment?

554. Have the supporting tools been developed or acquired?

555. Who should prepare the process improvement action plan?

556. Are you meeting the quality standards?

557. Are you making progress on the improvement framework?

558. The motive is determined by asking, Why do you want to achieve this goal?

559. What personnel are the change agents for your initiative?

560. Where are you now?

561. To elicit goal statements, do you ask a question such as, What do you want to achieve?

562. Purpose of goal: the motive is determined by asking, why do you want to achieve this goal?

563. What personnel are the sponsors for that initiative?

564. Why do you want to achieve the goal?

565. Are you following the quality standards?

566. Modeling current processes is great, and will you ever see a return on that investment?

567. What actions are needed to address the problems and achieve the goals?

2.27 Responsibility Assignment Matrix: Release Management

568. How can this help you with team building?

569. Too many rs: with too many people labeled as doing the work, are there too many hands involved?

570. Will too many Signing-off responsibilities delay the completion of the activity/deliverable?

571. Who is the Release Management project Manager?

572. Budgeted cost for work performed?

573. How cost benefit analysis?

574. Contemplated overhead expenditure for each period based on the best information currently available?

575. Competencies and craftsmanship – what competencies are necessary and what level?

576. What are some important Release Management project communications management tools?

577. Is the anticipated (firm and potential) business base Release Management projected in a rational, consistent manner?

578. Actual cost of work performed?

579. Are all authorized tasks assigned to identified organizational elements?

580. Are management actions taken to reduce indirect costs when there are significant adverse variances?

581. Changes in the overhead pool and/or organization structures?

582. Incurrence of actual indirect costs in excess of budgets, by element of expense?

583. Is work properly classified as measured effort, LOE, or apportioned effort and appropriately separated?

584. Does the scheduling system identify in a timely manner the status of work?

585. Is data disseminated to the contractors management timely, accurate, and usable?

2.28 Roles and Responsibilities: Release Management

586. Are Release Management project team roles and responsibilities identified and documented?

587. How well did the Release Management project Team understand the expectations of specific roles and responsibilities?

588. Have you ever been a part of this team?

589. What specific behaviors did you observe?

590. Authority: what areas/Release Management projects in your work do you have the authority to decide upon and act on the already stated decisions?

591. Do the values and practices inherent in the culture of your organization foster or hinder the process?

592. Are governance roles and responsibilities documented?

593. Once the responsibilities are defined for the Release Management project, have the deliverables, roles and responsibilities been clearly communicated to every participant?

594. To decide whether to use a quality measurement, ask how will you know when it is achieved?

595. Are Release Management project team roles and responsibilities identified and documented?

596. Implementation of actions: Who are the responsible units?

597. What is working well within your organizations performance management system?

598. Who is responsible for each task?

599. Required skills, knowledge, experience?

600. Where are you most strong as a supervisor?

601. Are the quality assurance functions and related roles and responsibilities clearly defined?

602. What should you do now to ensure that you are meeting all expectations of your current position?

603. What are your major roles and responsibilities in the area of performance measurement and assessment?

604. Concern: where are you limited or have no authority, where you can not influence?

605. What areas of supervision are challenging for you?

2.29 Human Resource Management Plan: Release Management

606. Does the Release Management project have a Quality Culture?

607. Has the schedule been baselined?

608. Does a documented Release Management project organizational policy & plan (i.e. governance model) exist?

609. Were Release Management project team members involved in the development of activity & task decomposition?

610. Are change requests logged and managed?

611. Are non-critical path items updated and agreed upon with the teams?

612. Were the budget estimates reasonable?

613. Have key stakeholders been identified?

614. Release Management project definition & scope?

615. Has a capability assessment been conducted?

616. Were decisions made in a timely manner?

617. Have all unresolved risks been documented?

618. Are people being developed to meet the challenges of the future?

619. What is this Release Management project aiming to achieve?

620. Are the right people being attracted and retained to meet the future challenges?

621. Are written status reports provided on a designated frequent basis?

622. Are target dates established for each milestone deliverable?

2.30 Communications Management Plan: Release Management

623. Who will use or be affected by the result of a Release Management project?

624. Who is the stakeholder?

625. Which stakeholders are thought leaders, influences, or early adopters?

626. What is the political influence?

627. How much time does it take to do it?

628. Who have you worked with in past, similar initiatives?

629. Can you think of other people who might have concerns or interests?

630. Why manage stakeholders?

631. What data is going to be required?

632. What approaches do you use?

633. Conflict resolution -which method when?

634. Do you have members of your team responsible for certain stakeholders?

635. Are there too many who have an interest in some

aspect of your work?

636. How is this initiative related to other portfolios, programs, or Release Management projects?

637. Are others needed?

638. Who to learn from?

639. Who needs to know and how much?

640. Who is responsible?

641. What are the interrelationships?

642. What is Release Management project communications management?

2.31 Risk Management Plan: Release Management

643. For software; are compilers and code generators available and suitable for the product to be built?

644. Have customers been involved fully in the definition of requirements?

645. Do benefits and chances of success outweigh potential damage if success is not attained?

646. Are staff committed for the duration of the product?

647. Do you manage the process through use of metrics?

648. Does the customer have a solid idea of what is required?

649. What did not work so well?

650. How is the audit profession changing?

651. Workarounds are determined during which step of risk management?

652. Is there anything you would now do differently on your Release Management project based on this experience?

653. Where are you confronted with risks during the

business phases?

654. Minimize cost and financial risk?

655. Have staff received necessary training?

656. What is the probability the risk avoidance strategy will be successful?

657. Do you have a mechanism for managing change?

658. Can you stabilize dynamic risk factors?

659. Are there risks to human health or the environment that need to be controlled or mitigated?

660. Are the best people available?

661. Which risks should get the attention?

662. What are some questions that should be addressed in a risk management plan?

2.32 Risk Register: Release Management

663. What could prevent you delivering on the strategic program objectives and what is being done to mitigate corresponding issues?

664. What are you going to do to limit the Release Management projects risk exposure due to the identified risks?

665. Risk categories: what are the main categories of risks that should be addressed on this Release Management project?

666. People risk -are people with appropriate skills available to help complete the Release Management project?

667. Can the likelihood and impact of failing to achieve corresponding recommendations and action plans be assessed?

668. What has changed since the last period?

669. Are corrective measures implemented as planned?

670. What should you do now?

671. What are the assumptions and current status that support the assessment of the risk?

672. Methodology: how will risk management be performed on this Release Management project?

673. What is the probability and impact of the risk occurring?

674. Are implemented controls working as others should?

675. What are your key risks/show istoppers and what is being done to manage them?

676. What are the main aims, objectives of the policy, strategy, or service and the intended outcomes?

677. How are risks graded?

678. What risks might negatively or positively affect achieving the Release Management project objectives?

679. Recovery actions - planned actions taken once a risk has occurred to allow you to move on. What should you do after?

680. Have other controls and solutions been implemented in other services which could be applied as an alternative to additional funding?

681. When is it going to be done?

682. What evidence do you have to justify the likelihood score of the risk (audit, incident report, claim, complaints, inspection, internal review)?

2.33 Probability and Impact Assessment: Release Management

683. Which of your Release Management projects should be selected when compared with other Release Management projects?

684. How is the risk management process used in practice?

685. Do you have specific methods that you use for each phase of the process?

686. What is the likely future demand of the customer?

687. What risks does your organization have if the Release Management projects fail to meet deadline?

688. Who should be notified of the occurrence of each of the risk indicators?

689. What are the channels available for distribution to the customer?

690. Risk categorization -which of your categories has more risk than others?

691. What are the chances the risk event will occur?

692. What should be done with non-critical risks?

693. Do you train all developers in the process?

694. What risks are necessary to achieve success?

695. What are the levels of understanding of the future users of the outcome/results of this Release Management project?

696. What are the likely future requirements?

697. What should be the requirement of organizational restructuring as each subRelease Management project goes through a different lifecycle phase?

698. Is the number of people on the Release Management project team adequate to do the job?

699. Will new information become available during the Release Management project?

2.34 Probability and Impact Matrix: Release Management

700. Are staff committed for the duration of the Release Management project?

701. Number of users of the product?

702. What will be the likely political environment during the life of the Release Management project?

703. Are some people working on multiple Release Management projects?

704. What is the industrial relations prevailing in this organization?

705. Risk may be made during which step of risk management?

706. Which should be probably done NEXT?

707. How would you assess the risk management process in the Release Management project?

708. Are you on schedule?

709. What are the current requirements of the customer?

710. Mandated specific features?

711. Is the customer willing to participate in reviews?

712. Brain storm – mind maps, what if?

713. How likely is the current plan to come in on schedule or on budget?

714. What is the likelihood of a breakthrough?

715. Non-valid or incredible information?

716. What are the uncertainties associated with the technology selected for the Release Management project?

717. How well were you able to manage your risk?

718. Amount of reused software?

2.35 Risk Data Sheet: Release Management

719. Is the data sufficiently specified in terms of the type of failure being analyzed, and its frequency or probability?

720. What are you weak at and therefore need to do better?

721. Who has a vested interest in how you perform as your organization (our stakeholders)?

722. What is the chance that it will happen?

723. How can it happen?

724. What was measured?

725. What can you do?

726. What do people affected think about the need for, and practicality of preventive measures?

727. If it happens, what are the consequences?

728. Are new hazards created?

729. What do you know?

730. During work activities could hazards exist?

731. What can happen?

732. Potential for recurrence?

733. What are the main opportunities available to you that you should grab while you can?

734. What actions can be taken to eliminate or remove risk?

735. How reliable is the data source?

736. What are you trying to achieve (Objectives)?

737. Type of risk identified?

738. Do effective diagnostic tests exist?

2.36 Procurement Management Plan: Release Management

739. Is there a formal set of procedures supporting Issues Management?

740. Has Release Management project success criteria been defined?

741. Are post milestone Release Management project reviews (PMPR) conducted with your organization at least once a year?

742. Have stakeholder accountabilities & responsibilities been clearly defined?

743. Are milestone deliverables effectively tracked and compared to Release Management project plan?

744. Does the business case include how the Release Management project aligns with your organizations strategic goals & objectives?

745. Are stakeholders aware and supportive of the principles and practices of modern software estimation?

746. Does the Release Management project have a Quality Culture?

747. What were things that you did very well and want to do the same again on the next Release Management project?

748. Are all resource assumptions documented?

749. Are parking lot items captured?

750. Is there a procurement management plan in place?

751. Are the Release Management project team members located locally to the users/stakeholders?

752. What are things that you need to improve?

753. Has the budget been baselined?

754. What is the last item a Release Management project manager must do to finalize Release Management project close-out?

755. What are you trying to accomplish?

2.37 Source Selection Criteria: Release Management

756. Is the offeror pricing what is technically proposed?

757. Do you ensure you evaluate what you asked for, not what you want to see or expect to see?

758. Are there any specific considerations that precludes offers from being selected as the awardee?

759. How much past performance information should be requested?

760. Is the contracting office likely to receive more purchase requests for this item or service during the coming year?

761. How do you encourage efficiency and consistency?

762. What management structure does your organization consider as optimal for performing the contract?

763. Are evaluators ready to begin this task?

764. Are resultant proposal revisions allowed?

765. How do you facilitate evaluation against published criteria?

766. What past performance information should be requested?

767. What will you use to capture evaluation and subsequent documentation?

768. Does your documentation identify why the team concurs or differs with reported performance from past performance report (CPARs, questionnaire responses, etc.)?

769. What documentation should be used to support the selection decision?

770. What does an evaluation address and what does a sample resemble?

771. How and when do you enter into Release Management project Procurement Management?

772. How should oral presentations be evaluated?

773. How are oral presentations documented?

774. Do you want to have them collaborate at subfactor level?

775. Does the evaluation of any change include an impact analysis; how will the change affect the scope, time, cost, and quality of the goods or services being provided?

2.38 Stakeholder Management Plan: Release Management

776. What is meant by activity dependencies and how do they relate to network diagramming?

777. Have external dependencies been captured in the schedule?

778. Why would you develop a Release Management project Execution Plan?

779. Detail warranty and/or maintenance periods?

780. Was your organizations estimating methodology being used and followed?

781. Where will verification occur, and by whom?

782. Are you meeting your customers expectations consistently?

783. Are the people assigned to the Release Management project sufficiently qualified?

784. Have activity relationships and interdependencies within tasks been adequately identified?

785. Are the Release Management project team members located locally to the users/stakeholders?

786. Is it standard practice to formally commit

stakeholders to the Release Management project via agreements?

787. Are communication systems currently in place appropriate?

788. Does the Release Management project have a Statement of Work?

789. Is Release Management project status reviewed with the steering and executive teams at appropriate intervals?

790. Is the performance of the supplier to be rated and documented?

791. Does the business case include how the Release Management project aligns with your organizations strategic goals & objectives?

2.39 Change Management Plan: Release Management

792. What goal(s) do you hope to accomplish?

793. What policies and procedures need to be changed?

794. How frequently should you repeat the message?

795. What are the specific target groups/audiences that will be impacted by this change?

796. How badly can information be misinterpreted?

797. Will the readiness criteria be met prior to the training roll out?

798. What prerequisite knowledge or training is required?

799. Is a training information sheet available?

800. Has the priority for this Release Management project been set by the Business Unit Management Team?

801. What new competencies will be required for the roles?

802. How will you deal with anger about the restricting of communications due to confidentiality considerations?

803. What type of materials/channels will be available to leverage?

804. What new roles are needed?

805. What can you do to minimise misinterpretation and negative perceptions?

806. What is going to be done differently?

807. How far reaching in your organization is the change?

808. What skills, education, knowledge, or work experiences should the resources have for each identified competency?

809. Have the business unit contacts been selected and notified?

810. What processes are in place to manage knowledge about the Release Management project?

3.0 Executing Process Group: Release Management

811. How do you enter durations, link tasks, and view critical path information?

812. Who will provide training?

813. What are the critical steps involved with strategy mapping?

814. Mitigate. what will you do to minimize the impact should a risk event occur?

815. What were things that you did well, and could improve, and how?

816. How could you control progress of your Release Management project?

817. Contingency planning. if a risk event occurs, what will you do?

818. Why should Release Management project managers strive to make jobs look easy?

819. What does it mean to take a systems view of a Release Management project?

820. Do schedule issues conflicts?

821. How can you use Microsoft Release Management project and Excel to assist in Release Management

project risk management?

822. In what way has the program come up with innovative measures for problem-solving?

823. After how many days will the lease cost be the same as the purchase cost for the equipment?

824. What were things that you need to improve?

825. On which process should team members spend the most time?

826. Would you rate yourself as being risk-averse, risk-neutral, or risk-seeking?

827. What are the Release Management project management deliverables of each process group?

828. Could a new application negatively affect the current IT infrastructure?

3.1 Team Member Status Report: Release Management

829. How it is to be done?

830. Are your organizations Release Management projects more successful over time?

831. Does the product, good, or service already exist within your organization?

832. Do you have an Enterprise Release Management project Management Office (EPMO)?

833. Is there evidence that staff is taking a more professional approach toward management of your organizations Release Management projects?

834. The problem with Reward & Recognition Programs is that the truly deserving people all too often get left out. How can you make it practical?

835. Are the products of your organizations Release Management projects meeting customers objectives?

836. Why is it to be done?

837. What specific interest groups do you have in place?

838. How does this product, good, or service meet the needs of the Release Management project and your organization as a whole?

839. Does your organization have the means (staff, money, contract, etc.) to produce or to acquire the product, good, or service?

840. How can you make it practical?

841. When a teams productivity and success depend on collaboration and the efficient flow of information, what generally fails them?

842. Are the attitudes of staff regarding Release Management project work improving?

843. Will the staff do training or is that done by a third party?

844. How will resource planning be done?

845. Does every department have to have a Release Management project Manager on staff?

846. How much risk is involved?

847. What is to be done?

3.2 Change Request: Release Management

848. How well do experienced software developers predict software change?

849. How are the measures for carrying out the change established?

850. Are there requirements attributes that are strongly related to the complexity and size?

851. Who is communicating the change?

852. How is quality being addressed on the Release Management project?

853. Will all change requests and current status be logged?

854. Has a formal technical review been conducted to assess technical correctness?

855. Who is responsible for the implementation and monitoring of all measures?

856. Who can suggest changes?

857. Is it feasible to use requirements attributes as predictors of reliability?

858. What are the basic mechanics of the Change Advisory Board (CAB)?

859. What needs to be communicated?

860. Have all related configuration items been properly updated?

861. Customer acceptance plan how will the customer verify the change has been implemented successfully?

862. Has the change been highlighted and documented in the CSCI?

863. What is the function of the change control committee?

864. Who is responsible to authorize changes?

865. Who has responsibility for approving and ranking changes?

866. How does a team identify the discrete elements of a configuration?

3.3 Change Log: Release Management

867. Is the change backward compatible without limitations?

868. Is the change request within Release Management project scope?

869. When was the request submitted?

870. Is the change request open, closed or pending?

871. When was the request approved?

872. Who initiated the change request?

873. Do the described changes impact on the integrity or security of the system?

874. How does this change affect the timeline of the schedule?

875. How does this change affect scope?

876. How does this relate to the standards developed for specific business processes?

877. Is this a mandatory replacement?

878. Is the submitted change a new change or a modification of a previously approved change?

879. Will the Release Management project fail if the change request is not executed?

880. Is the requested change request a result of changes in other Release Management project(s)?

881. Should a more thorough impact analysis be conducted?

3.4 Decision Log: Release Management

882. Behaviors; what are guidelines that the team has identified that will assist them with getting the most out of team meetings?

883. How does provision of information, both in terms of content and presentation, influence acceptance of alternative strategies?

884. Linked to original objective?

885. How does the use a Decision Support System influence the strategies/tactics or costs?

886. Decision-making process; how will the team make decisions?

887. What is the average size of your matters in an applicable measurement?

888. What alternatives/risks were considered?

889. What is your overall strategy for quality control / quality assurance procedures?

890. How consolidated and comprehensive a story can you tell by capturing currently available incident data in a central location and through a log of key decisions during an incident?

891. What is the line where eDiscovery ends and

document review begins?

892. What makes you different or better than others companies selling the same thing?

893. How do you know when you are achieving it?

894. What eDiscovery problem or issue did your organization set out to fix or make better?

895. Who is the decisionmaker?

896. Does anything need to be adjusted?

897. Is your opponent open to a non-traditional workflow, or will it likely challenge anything you do?

898. Is everything working as expected?

899. How do you define success?

900. Which variables make a critical difference?

901. Meeting purpose; why does this team meet?

3.5 Quality Audit: Release Management

902. How does your organization know that the quality of its supervisors is appropriately effective and constructive?

903. Are the intentions consistent with external obligations (such as applicable laws)?

904. Do prior clients have a positive opinion of your organization?

905. How does your organization know that its range of activities are being reviewed as rigorously and constructively as they could be?

906. How does your organization know that the system for managing its facilities is appropriately effective and constructive?

907. How does your organization know that its system for commercializing research outputs is appropriately effective and constructive?

908. How does your organization know that its research funding systems are appropriately effective and constructive in enabling quality research outcomes?

909. How does your organization know that it is appropriately effective and constructive in preparing its staff for organizational aspirations?

910. How does your organization know that its security arrangements are appropriately effective and constructive?

911. Health and safety arrangements; stress management workshops. How does your organization know that it provides a safe and healthy environment?

912. How does your organization know that the research supervision provided to its staff is appropriately effective and constructive?

913. How are you auditing your organizations compliance with regulations?

914. Is your organizational structure established and each positions responsibility defined?

915. How does your organization know that its management of its ethical responsibilities is appropriately effective and constructive?

916. Are adequate and conveniently located toilet facilities available for use by the employees?

917. How does your organization know that its risk management system is appropriately effective and constructive?

918. If your organization thinks it is doing something well, can it prove this?

919. How does your organization know that its system for attending to the particular needs of its international staff is appropriately effective and

constructive?

920. How does your organization know that its advisory services are appropriately effective and constructive?

921. Are training programs documented?

3.6 Team Directory: Release Management

922. Process decisions: do job conditions warrant additional actions to collect job information and document on-site activity?

923. Who will write the meeting minutes and distribute?

924. Process decisions: are contractors adequately prosecuting the work?

925. How does the team resolve conflicts and ensure tasks are completed?

926. Where will the product be used and/or delivered or built when appropriate?

927. Who is the Sponsor?

928. Is construction on schedule?

929. Process decisions: is work progressing on schedule and per contract requirements?

930. Have you decided when to celebrate the Release Management projects completion date?

931. When will you produce deliverables?

932. Process decisions: are all start-up, turn over and close out requirements of the contract satisfied?

933. Contract requirements complied with?

934. Who are the Team Members?

935. Decisions: what could be done better to improve the quality of the constructed product?

936. Process decisions: do invoice amounts match accepted work in place?

937. Where should the information be distributed?

938. How will you accomplish and manage the objectives?

939. Timing: when do the effects of communication take place?

3.7 Team Operating Agreement: Release Management

940. How will you divide work equitably?

941. Do you vary your voice pace, tone and pitch to engage participants and gain involvement?

942. Did you recap the meeting purpose, time, and expectations?

943. What is the number of cases currently teamed?

944. Do you post meeting notes and the recording (if used) and notify participants?

945. Has the appropriate access to relevant data and analysis capability been granted?

946. What are the boundaries (organizational or geographic) within which you operate?

947. Do you record meetings for the already stated unable to attend?

948. How do you want to be thought of and known within your organization?

949. To whom do you deliver your services?

950. The method to be used in the decision making process; Will it be consensus, majority rule, or the supervisor having the final say?

951. Does your team need access to all documents and information at all times?

952. What is culture?

953. What types of accommodations will be formulated and put in place for sustaining the team?

954. Do you ask participants to close laptops and place mobile devices on silent on the table while the meeting is in progress?

955. Do you prevent individuals from dominating the meeting?

956. Do you ensure that all participants know how to use the required technology?

957. What are the safety issues/risks that need to be addressed and/or that the team needs to consider?

958. Are there more than two functional areas represented by your team?

959. Do you begin with a question to engage everyone?

3.8 Team Performance Assessment: Release Management

960. Do friends perform better than acquaintances?

961. Delaying market entry: how long is too long?

962. To what degree does the teams work approach provide opportunity for members to engage in results-based evaluation?

963. To what degree will the team ensure that all members equitably share the work essential to the success of the team?

964. To what degree will the team adopt a concrete, clearly understood, and agreed-upon approach that will result in achievement of the teams goals?

965. Can familiarity breed backup?

966. Effects of crew composition on crew performance: Does the whole equal the sum of its parts?

967. To what degree are the goals realistic?

968. To what degree is the team cognizant of small wins to be celebrated along the way?

969. To what degree does the teams purpose constitute a broader, deeper aspiration than just accomplishing short-term goals?

970. What do you think is the most constructive thing that could be done now to resolve considerations and disputes about method variance?

971. To what degree does the teams work approach provide opportunity for members to engage in fact-based problem solving?

972. To what degree do team members feel that the purpose of the team is important, if not exciting?

973. To what degree are the members clear on what they are individually responsible for and what they are jointly responsible for?

974. How much interpersonal friction is there in your team?

975. To what degree do members articulate the goals beyond the team membership?

976. When a reviewer complains about method variance, what is the essence of the complaint?

977. To what degree do members understand and articulate the same purpose without relying on ambiguous abstractions?

978. To what degree will the approach capitalize on and enhance the skills of all team members in a manner that takes into consideration other demands on members of the team?

979. To what degree are the relative importance and priority of the goals clear to all team members?

3.9 Team Member Performance Assessment: Release Management

980. Does the rater (supervisor) have the authority or responsibility to tell an employee that the employees performance is unsatisfactory?

981. How do you make use of research?

982. Does platform-specific assessment information contribute to training placement or tailoring of instruction (e.g. aptitude-treatment interaction)?

983. To what degree are the goals ambitious?

984. Should a ratee get a copy of all the raters documents about the employees performance?

985. To what degree can the team measure progress against specific goals?

986. To what degree do the goals specify concrete team work products?

987. What, if any, steps are available for employees who feel they have been unfairly or inaccurately rated?

988. What specific plans do you have for developing effective cross-platform assessments in a blended learning environment?

989. To what degree do team members articulate the

teams work approach?

990. How do you work together to improve teaching and learning?

991. Does statute or regulation require the job responsibility?

992. How accurately is your plan implemented?

993. How was the determination made for which training platforms would be used (i.e., media selection)?

994. To what degree can team members meet frequently enough to accomplish the teams ends?

995. To what degree will new and supplemental skills be introduced as the need is recognized?

996. What types of learning are targeted (e.g., cognitive, affective, psychomotor, procedural)?

997. How will they be formed?

998. Who should attend?

3.10 Issue Log: Release Management

999. Are there common objectives between the team and the stakeholder?

1000. What approaches to you feel are the best ones to use?

1001. Where do team members get information?

1002. How were past initiatives successful?

1003. How do you manage human resources?

1004. What are the typical contents?

1005. Who reported the issue?

1006. Why do you manage communications?

1007. Are they needed?

1008. Are the Release Management project issues uniquely identified, including to which product they refer?

1009. Can an impact cause deviation beyond team, stage or Release Management project tolerances?

1010. Are there potential barriers between the team and the stakeholder?

1011. Persistence; will users learn a work around or will they be bothered every time?

1012. Is access to the Issue Log controlled?

1013. What does the stakeholder need from the team?

1014. In classifying stakeholders, which approach to do so are you using?

4.0 Monitoring and Controlling Process Group: Release Management

1015. What are the deliverables?

1016. Is progress on outcomes due to your program?

1017. Is the program making progress in helping to achieve the set results?

1018. How well did the chosen processes produce the expected results?

1019. Use: how will they use the information?

1020. How is agile portfolio management done?

1021. When will the Release Management project be done?

1022. Is there sufficient funding available for this?

1023. How many potential communications channels exist on the Release Management project?

1024. Is the program in place as intended?

1025. How many more potential communications channels were introduced by the discovery of the new stakeholders?

1026. How well did you do?

1027. If a risk event occurs, what will you do?

1028. Who needs to be involved in the planning?

1029. Purpose: toward what end is the evaluation being conducted?

1030. How to ensure validity, quality and consistency?

4.1 Project Performance Report: Release Management

1031. To what degree are the teams goals and objectives clear, simple, and measurable?

1032. To what degree do the structures of the formal organization motivate taskrelevant behavior and facilitate task completion?

1033. To what degree can the cognitive capacity of individuals accommodate the flow of information?

1034. To what degree do team members frequently explore the teams purpose and its implications?

1035. To what degree are the skill areas critical to team performance present?

1036. To what degree does the informal organization make use of individual resources and meet individual needs?

1037. To what degree does the information network provide individuals with the information they require?

1038. To what degree will each member have the opportunity to advance his or her professional skills in all three of the above categories while contributing to the accomplishment of the teams purpose and goals?

1039. What degree are the relative importance and priority of the goals clear to all team members?

1040. To what degree are fresh input and perspectives systematically caught and added (for example, through information and analysis, new members, and senior sponsors)?

1041. To what degree does the information network communicate information relevant to the task?

1042. To what degree do individual skills and abilities match task demands?

1043. To what degree is the information network consistent with the structure of the formal organization?

4.2 Variance Analysis: Release Management

1044. Are work packages assigned to performing organizations?

1045. Who are responsible for overhead performance control of related costs?

1046. Is the market likely to continue to grow at this rate next year?

1047. Did an existing competitor change strategy?

1048. How do you identify and isolate causes of favorable and unfavorable cost and schedule variances?

1049. What does a favorable labor efficiency variance mean?

1050. Are there externalities from having some customers, even if they are unprofitable in the short run?

1051. Are all cwbs elements specified for external reporting?

1052. Do you identify potential or actual budget-based and time-based schedule variances?

1053. How do you evaluate the impact of schedule changes, work around, et?

1054. What are the actual costs to date?

1055. Are all elements of indirect expense identified to overhead cost budgets of Release Management projections?

1056. How do you haverify authorization to proceed with all authorized work?

1057. Are all budgets assigned to control accounts?

1058. Contract line items and end items?

1059. Other relevant issues of Variance Analysis -selling price or gross margin?

1060. How do you manage changes in the nature of the overhead requirements?

1061. Are material costs reported within the same period as that in which BCWP is earned for that material?

4.3 Earned Value Status: Release Management

1062. What is the unit of forecast value?

1063. Are you hitting your Release Management projects targets?

1064. Where is evidence-based earned value in your organization reported?

1065. Verification is a process of ensuring that the developed system satisfies the stakeholders agreements and specifications; Are you building the product right? What do you haverify?

1066. Validation is a process of ensuring that the developed system will actually achieve the stakeholders desired outcomes; Are you building the right product? What do you validate?

1067. Earned value can be used in almost any Release Management project situation and in almost any Release Management project environment. it may be used on large Release Management projects, medium sized Release Management projects, tiny Release Management projects (in cut-down form), complex and simple Release Management projects and in any market sector. some people, of course, know all about earned value, they have used it for years - but perhaps not as effectively as they could have?

1068. How much is it going to cost by the finish?

1069. How does this compare with other Release Management projects?

1070. Where are your problem areas?

1071. If earned value management (EVM) is so good in determining the true status of a Release Management project and Release Management project its completion, why is it that hardly any one uses it in information systems related Release Management projects?

1072. When is it going to finish?

4.4 Risk Audit: Release Management

1073. Does the customer understand the process?

1074. Do all coaches/instructors/leaders have appropriate and current accreditation?

1075. Are all participants informed of safety issues?

1076. Are contracts reviewed before renewal?

1077. Extending the consideration on the halo effect, to what extent are auditors able to build skepticism in evidence review?

1078. Are you aware of the industry standards that apply to your operations?

1079. Where will the next scandal or adverse media involving your organization come from?

1080. Do you conduct risk assessments on all programs, activities and events?

1081. Strategic business risk audit methodologies; are corresponding an attempt to sell other services, and is management becoming the client of the audit rather than the shareholder?

1082. Does willful intent modify risk-based auditing?

1083. What are the legal implications of not identifying a complete universe of business risks?

1084. Can analytical tests provide evidence that is as strong as evidence from traditional substantive tests?

1085. Are Release Management project requirements stable?

1086. Have reasonable steps been taken to reduce the risks to acceptable levels?

1087. Are there any forms the staff is required to sign?

1088. How are risk appetites expressed?

1089. Have all involved been advised of any obligations they have to sponsors?

1090. What risk does not having unique identification present?

4.5 Contractor Status Report: Release Management

1091. What are the minimum and optimal bandwidth requirements for the proposed soluiton?

1092. What process manages the contracts?

1093. How long have you been using the services?

1094. Are there contractual transfer concerns?

1095. Describe how often regular updates are made to the proposed solution. Are corresponding regular updates included in the standard maintenance plan?

1096. What was the final actual cost?

1097. What was the actual budget or estimated cost for your organizations services?

1098. How does the proposed individual meet each requirement?

1099. What is the average response time for answering a support call?

1100. What was the overall budget or estimated cost?

1101. How is risk transferred?

1102. If applicable; describe your standard schedule for new software version releases. Are new software version releases included in the standard maintenance plan?

1103. What was the budget or estimated cost for your organizations services?

1104. Who can list a Release Management project as organization experience, your organization or a previous employee of your organization?

4.6 Formal Acceptance: Release Management

1105. Was business value realized?

1106. Does it do what client said it would?

1107. Did the Release Management project achieve its MOV?

1108. Do you buy-in installation services?

1109. How well did the team follow the methodology?

1110. What function(s) does it fill or meet?

1111. Who would use it?

1112. Was the Release Management project goal achieved?

1113. What features, practices, and processes proved to be strengths or weaknesses?

1114. Did the Release Management project manager and team act in a professional and ethical manner?

1115. General estimate of the costs and times to complete the Release Management project?

1116. What can you do better next time?

1117. What is the Acceptance Management Process?

1118. Who supplies data?

1119. How does your team plan to obtain formal acceptance on your Release Management project?

1120. Do you buy pre-configured systems or build your own configuration?

1121. What lessons were learned about your Release Management project management methodology?

1122. Was the Release Management project managed well?

1123. Do you perform formal acceptance or burn-in tests?

1124. Was the client satisfied with the Release Management project results?

5.0 Closing Process Group: Release Management

1125. How well defined and documented were the Release Management project management processes you chose to use?

1126. What is the Release Management project name and date of completion?

1127. Is this a follow-on to a previous Release Management project?

1128. Who are the Release Management project stakeholders?

1129. Is there a clear cause and effect between the activity and the lesson learned?

1130. What were the actual outcomes?

1131. Were cost budgets met?

1132. Did the Release Management project team have the right skills?

1133. What areas were overlooked on this Release Management project?

1134. What could have been improved?

1135. Was the user/client satisfied with the end product?

1136. Is the Release Management project funded?

1137. What will you do?

1138. Will the Release Management project deliverable(s) replace a current asset or group of assets?

1139. What communication items need improvement?

5.1 Procurement Audit: Release Management

1140. Was the overall procurement done within a reasonable time?

1141. Is the functioning of automatic disbursement programs tested by an independent party?

1142. Is your organization policy on purchasing covered by a written manual?

1143. Was the formal review of requests to participate or evaluation of bids correctly undertaken?

1144. Are buyers rotated so that they do not deal with the same vendors year in and year out?

1145. Are there established procedures for dealing with and documenting non-performance and return of goods?

1146. Has the department identified and described the different elements in the procurement process?

1147. Are internal control mechanisms performed before payments?

1148. Is confidentiality guaranteed during the whole process?

1149. Are requisitions and other purchase requests batched to reduce the number of orders issued?

1150. Has alternatives been considered for the specified procurement Release Management project?

1151. How is the evaluation of contract performance organized?

1152. Did your organization identify the full contract value and include options and provisions for renewals?

1153. Were the performance conditions under the contract comprehensive and unambiguous?

1154. Are there mechanisms for evaluating the departments suppliers performance in relation to prices, quality, delivery and innovation?

1155. Is it tested periodically, whether your organizations way of handling tasks is competitive in relation to price and quality?

1156. Are there mechanisms in place to evaluate the performance of the departments suppliers?

1157. Are there systems for recording and monitoring in order to discover malpractice and fraud in the procurement function/unit?

1158. Were products/services not received within the prescribed time limit?

1159. Where required, did candidates give evidence of complying with quality assurance standards?

5.2 Contract Close-Out: Release Management

1160. What happens to the recipient of services?

1161. Have all contracts been closed?

1162. Was the contract sufficiently clear so as not to result in numerous disputes and misunderstandings?

1163. Change in attitude or behavior?

1164. Why Outsource?

1165. Has each contract been audited to verify acceptance and delivery?

1166. Have all acceptance criteria been met prior to final payment to contractors?

1167. Have all contracts been completed?

1168. Change in circumstances?

1169. How is the contracting office notified of the automatic contract close-out?

1170. Are the signers the authorized officials?

1171. Was the contract complete without requiring numerous changes and revisions?

1172. Was the contract type appropriate?

1173. What is capture management?

1174. Parties: Authorized?

1175. Parties: who is involved?

1176. How does it work?

1177. Change in knowledge?

1178. How/when used ?

1179. Have all contract records been included in the Release Management project archives?

5.3 Project or Phase Close-Out: Release Management

1180. What could be done to improve the process?

1181. Complete yes or no?

1182. What was learned?

1183. Who exerted influence that has positively affected or negatively impacted the Release Management project?

1184. What are the informational communication needs for each stakeholder?

1185. Which changes might a stakeholder be required to make as a result of the Release Management project?

1186. What is a Risk Management Process?

1187. What is a Risk?

1188. Did the Release Management project management methodology work?

1189. Does the lesson educate others to improve performance?

1190. Planned remaining costs?

1191. What are they?

1192. What advantages do the an individual interview have over a group meeting, and vice-versa?

1193. What can you do better next time, and what specific actions can you take to improve?

1194. What security considerations needed to be addressed during the procurement life cycle?

1195. What is this stakeholder expecting?

1196. Is the lesson significant, valid, and applicable?

5.4 Lessons Learned: Release Management

1197. Were the Release Management project objectives met (if not, briefly account for what wasnt met)?

1198. How effective was the acceptance management process?

1199. How effective was the support you received during implementation of the product/service?

1200. Is the lesson based on actual Release Management project experience rather than on independent research?

1201. How effective were the techniques used to prepare you and your organization for the impact of the changes brought about by the product or service produced by the Release Management project?

1202. How many government and contractor personnel are authorized for the Release Management project?

1203. Was the purpose of the Release Management project, the end products and success criteria clearly defined and agreed at the start?

1204. If you had to do this Release Management project again, what is the one thing that you would change (related to process, not to technical solutions)?

1205. How to write up the lesson identified – how will you document the results of your analysis corresponding that you have an li ready to take the next step in the ll process?

1206. Overall, how effective was the performance of the Release Management project Manager?

1207. How comprehensive was integration testing?

1208. How effective was the documentation that you received with the Release Management project product/service?

1209. For the next Release Management project, how could you improve on the way Release Management project was conducted?

1210. What was the methodology behind successful learning experiences, and how might they be applied to the broader challenge of your organizations knowledge management?

1211. What were the most significant issues on this Release Management project?

1212. Under what legal authority did your organization head and program manager direct your organization and Release Management project?

1213. What was the single greatest success and the single greatest shortcoming or challenge from the Release Management projects perspective?

1214. Who had fiscal authority to manage the funding for the Release Management project, did that work?

1215. What was the geopolitical history during the origin of your organization and at the time of task input?

Index